John C. Crotts
Dimitrios Buhalis
Roger March
Editors

Global Alliances in Tourism and Hospitality Management

Global Alliances in Tourism and Hospitality Management has been co-published simultaneously as *International Journal of Hospitality & Tourism Administration,* Volume 1, Number 1 2000.

Pre-publicationt
REVIEWS,
COMMENTARIES,
EVALUATIONS . . .

"**T**his volume recognises the wealth of experience within the sector and brings the reader up to date with current developments. The papers add to our knowledge by looking widely beyond the tourism sector in their attempts to better explain and predict performance within the sector. At the same time, the qualities of the papers demonstrate the leading edge of tourism academics and practitioners in moving the development of strategic alliances forward. In this volume, the reader will gain a thorough understanding of the current nature of tourism strategic alliances. Well informed research offers academics and practitioners insights into how they can be improved further."

Adrian Palmer, PhD
Professor of Tourism Marketing
University of Ulster
Northern Ireland

More pre-publication
REVIEWS, COMMENTARIES, EVALUATIONS . . .

"**I**n a competitive business world companies recognise a need to improve service to customers in order to survive. Yet in many instances such improvements may require product enhancement which goes beyond the core business of the company. One way to address this is to form strategic alliances. This is just as true of tourism as in other industries, and indeed package holidays and airline alliances are largely built upon this concept. This book explores the problems and opportunities presented by such network building. In doing so, it not only examines the above mentioned alliances but also examines new forms of networks that have emerged, for example between the wine industry and tourism. It also includes the human resource management issues that arise from multinational work forces. In a series of case studies based on research, the editors have assembled a series of situations that provide insights, frameworks and structured understandings of inter- and intra-industry network buildings that will be of help to those interested in not only tourism but corporate strategy, distribution channels and marketing. It will thus appeal to a wide readership."

Professor Chris Ryan, BSc (Econ) Hons MEd, MPhil, PhD, NZITT
Waikato Management School
University of Waikato
Hamilton, New Zealand

Global Alliances
in Tourism and Hospitality
Management

Global Alliances in Tourism and Hospitality Management has been co-published simultaneously as *International Journal of Hospitality & Tourism Administration,* Volume 1, Number 1 2000.

The *International Journal of Hospitality & Tourism Administration* Monographic "Separates"

Below is a list of "separates," which in serials librarianship means a special issue simultaneously published as a special journal issue or double-issue *and* as a "separate" hardbound monograph. (This is a format which we also call a "DocuSerial.")

"Separates" are published because specialized libraries or professionals may wish to purchase a specific thematic issue by itself in a format which can be separately cataloged and shelved, as opposed to purchasing the journal on an on-going basis. Faculty members may also more easily consider a "separate" for classroom adoption.

"Separates" are carefully classified separately with the major book jobbers so that the journal tie-in can be noted on new book order slips to avoid duplicate purchasing.

You may wish to visit Haworth's Website at . . .

http://www.haworthpressinc.com

. . . to search our online catalog for complete tables of contents of these separates and related publications.

You may also call 1-800-HAWORTH (outside US/Canada: 607-722-5857), or Fax 1-800-895-0582 (outside US/Canada: 607-771-0012), or e-mail at:

getinfo@haworthpressinc.com

Global Alliances in Tourism and Hospitality Management, edited by John C. Crotts, Dimitrios Buhalis, and Roger March (Vol. 1, No. 1, 2000). *Provides you with the skills and strategies to build and create successful alliances in the hospitality and tourism fields. International in scope, this informative guide will help marketers, managers, and other professionals in the hospitality industry to lower company costs, raise profits, and gain strategic advantages in diversified markets.*

Global Alliances
in Tourism and Hospitality
Management

John C. Crotts
Dimitrios Buhalis
Roger March
Editors

Global Alliances in Tourism and Hospitality Management has been co-published simultaneously as *International Journal of Hospitality & Tourism Administration,* Volume 1, Number 1 2000.

The Haworth Hospitality Press
An Imprint of
The Haworth Press, Inc.
New York • London • Oxford

Published by

The Haworth Hospitality Press, 10 Alice Street, Binghamton, NY 13904-1580 USA

The Haworth Hospitality Press is an imprint of The Haworth Press, Inc., 10 Alice Street, Binghamton, NY 13904-1580 USA.

Global Alliances in Tourism and Hospitality Management has been co-published simultaneously as *International Journal of Hospitality & Tourism Administration,* Volume 1, Number 1 2000.

The development, preparation, and publication of this work has been undertaken with great care. However, the publisher, employees, editors, and agents of The Haworth Press and all imprints of The Haworth Press, Inc., including The Haworth Medical Press® and Pharmaceutical Products Press®, are not responsible for any errors contained herein or for consequences that may ensue from use of materials or information contained in this work. Opinions expressed by the author(s) are not necessarily those of The Haworth Press, Inc.

Cover design by Thomas J. Mayshock Jr.

Library of Congress Cataloging-in-Publication Data

Global alliances in tourism and hospitality management / John C. Crotts, Dimitrios Buhalis, Roger March, editors.
     p. cm.
     ". . . has been co-published simultaneously as International journal of hospitality & tourism administration, volume 1, number 1, 2000."
    Includes index.
    ISBN 0-7890-0783-5.–ISBN 0-7890-0818-1 (pbk. : alk. paper)
    1. Tourism. 2. Hospitality industry. I. Crotts, John C. II. Buhalis, Dimitrios. III. March, Roger.
G155.A1G4875 1999
338.4'791–dc21

99-38667
CIP

INDEXING & ABSTRACTING

Contributions to this publication are selectively indexed or abstracted in print, electronic, online, or CD-ROM version(s) of the reference tools and information services listed below. This list is current as of the copyright date of this publication. See the end of this section for additional notes.

- *Asian-Pacific Economic Literature*
- *AURSI African Urban & Regional Science Index*
- *Australian Business Index, The*
- *BUBL Information Service, An Internet-based Information Service for the UK higher education community <URL: http://bubl.ac.uk/>*
- *Centre des Hautes Etudes Touristiques (CHET)*
- *CNPIEC Reference Guide: Chinese National Directory of Foreign Periodicals*
- *FRANCIS, INISIST-CNRS*
- *Index to Periodical Articles Related to Law*
- *Leisure, Recreation, and Tourism Abstracts, c/o CAB International/CAB ACCESS. . . available in print, diskettes updated weekly, and on INTERNET. Providing full bibliographic listings, author affiliation, augmented keyword searching*
- *Lodging, Restaurant & Tourism Index*
- *PAIS (Public Affairs Information Service) NYC (www.pais.org)*
- *Public Affairs Information Service, Inc.*
- *Referativinyi Zhurnal (Abstracts Journal of the All-Russian Institute of Scientific and Technical Information)*
- *Sociological Abstracts (SA)*
- *"Travel Research Bookshelf" a current awareness service of the "Journal of Travel Research," published by the Travel & Tourism Association, Business Research Division, University of Colorado, Boulder, CO 80309-0420*
- *TURIZAM*

(continued)

Special Bibliographic Notes related to special journal issues
(separates) and indexing/abstracting:

- indexing/abstracting services in this list will also cover material in any "separate" that is co-published simultaneously with Haworth's special thematic journal issue or DocuSerial. Indexing/abstracting usually covers material at the article/chapter level.
- monographic co-editions are intended for either non-subscribers or libraries which intend to purchase a second copy for their circulating collections.
- monographic co-editions are reported to all jobbers/wholesalers/approval plans. The source journal is listed as the "series" to assist the prevention of duplicate purchasing in the same manner utilized for books-in-series.
- to facilitate user/access services all indexing/abstracting services are encouraged to utilize the co-indexing entry note indicated at the bottom of the first page of each article/chapter/contribution.
- this is intended to assist a library user of any reference tool (whether print, electronic, online, or CD-ROM) to locate the monographic version if the library has purchased this version but not a subscription to the source journal.
- individual articles/chapters in any Haworth publication are also available through the Haworth Document Delivery Service (HDDS).

Global Alliances in Tourism and Hospitality Management

CONTENTS

ABOUT THE EDITORS

John C. Crotts is Associate Professor and Director of the Hospitality and Tourism Management Program of the School of Business and Economics, at the College of Charleston. He has also been a visiting researcher at the Bornholm Research Centre in Denmark, a lecturer of the Tourism Centre at Otago University, Dunedin, New Zealand and Director of the Center for Tourism Research and Development at the University of Florida. His research encompasses the areas of economic psychology, tourism marketing strategy, and management of cooperative alliances. In addition to serving as the editor of *International Journal of Hospitality & Tourism Administration*, he also serves on the editorial board of the *Journal of Travel & Tourism Marketing* and the *Pacific Area Tourism Review*.

Dimitrios Buhalis is Senior Lecturer in Tourism at the University of Westminster and visiting faculty in several European Universities. He is also Chair of the Association of Tourism Teachers and Trainers and Committee Member of the International Federation of Information Technology and Tourism. He has chaired the ENTER 1998, 1999 and 2000 conferences and is a consultant to the World Tourism Organisation.

Roger March is Lecturer in Tourism Marketing, University of New South Wales, Sydney, Australia and Executive Director, Inbound Tourism Studies Centre. He has done extensive consulting work on the Asian and Japanese tourism markets. Clients have included Qantas Airways, Australian Tourist Commission, Tourism New South Wales, and the Inbound Tour Organisation of Australia (ITOA).

Introduction:
Global Alliances in Tourism and Hospitality Management

John C. Crotts
Dimitrios Buhalis
Roger March

INTRODUCTION

The development and management of alliances is a critical strategic skill in hospitality and tourism. Very little can happen in these sectors without multiple firms working collaboratively with one another to serve the consumer. All over the world companies are entering into alliances (see Table 1). However, research in this and other sectors suggest that most will fail leaving both partners sadder but hopefully the wiser. In this volume we will examine the basic elements of successful alliances–as well as those not so successful–and provide insights as to how to get ready to partner.

The words strategic alliances, relationships, strategic partnerships, and joint ventures all describe the coming together of two firms into a deliberate association that has some synergistic strategic value. They may assume the form of: (a) a buyer-seller relationship as in the case of an association meeting planner and a conference hotel, a restaurant and a single-source wholesale

John C. Crotts is Associate Professor and Director, Hospitality and Tourism Management Program, Department of Marketing and Management, School of Business and Economics, College of Charleston, Charleston, SC.

Dimitrios Buhalis is Senior Lecturer in Tourism, University of Westminster, London, England.

Roger March is affiliated with the School of Marketing, University of New South Wales, Sydney, Australia.

[Haworth co-indexing entry note]: "Introduction: Global Alliances in Tourism and Hospitality Management." Crotts, John C., Dimitrios Buhalis, and Roger March. Co-published simultaneously in *International Journal of Hospitality & Tourism Administration* (The Haworth Press, Inc.) Vol. 1, No. 1, 2000, pp. 1-10; and: *Global Alliances in Tourism and Hospitality Management* (ed: John C. Crotts, Dimitrios Buhalis, and Roger March) The Haworth Press, Inc., 2000, pp. 1-10. Single or multiple copies of this article are available for a fee from The Haworth Document Delivery Service [1-800-342-9678, 9:00 a.m. - 5:00 p.m. (EST). E-mail address: getinfo@haworthpressinc.com].

TABLE 1. Announcements of Alliances in the Travel Trade Press

---

*United, Lufthansa, Air Canada, SAS and THAI create Star Alliance
to bring benefits for airline customers*

*Northwest and Continental airlines form strategic alliance
to strengthen their position in a competitive global marketplace.
United-Delta consider similar move.*

*The Thomas Cook Group Ltd. forms a joint marketing alliance
with the American Automobile Association*

*The SABRE Group, ABACUS International Holdings Create Joint
Venture to Serve Asia-Pacific Travel Market: 7,300 Travel Agencies
to Use Customized SABRE System*

*ITT Sheraton and Visa U.S.A. Establish Marketing Relationship
That Benefits Travelers*

WorldRes Forms Strategic Alliance with the Pembridge Group

*Biztravel.com To Partner With EventSource; Alliance To Provide
First Integrated Event Planning and Business Travel Solution*

*Galileo International Teams Up with ITN
for Corporate Travel Solution*

WorldRes and Wizcom Announce Internet Alliance

*Equity Inns Enters Into Strategic Alliance
With U.S. Franchise Systems*

*California Cultural Tourism Coalition Debuts Multi-Million
Dollar Promotional Campaign 'California, Culture's Edge'*

Source: Hotel.Online Hospitality News Headlines

---

supplier; (b) a supplier-distributor relationship as in the case of airlines and retail travel agencies; (c) an alliance between two or more suppliers like the United-Lufthansa-Air Canada-SAS alliance; and (d) a joint venture between two companies like The SABRE Group and ABACUS International joint venture. All of these alliances share a sufficient amount of common elements that they can be treated as a basic unit of analysis. In the current competitive environment where firms strive to become world class competitors, the motivation to partner, in one or all of these forms, is great.

Since Thomas Cook packaged the first tour in 1841, hospitality and tourism enterprises have forged long term alliances with one another. Why are these alliances different today? To illustrate, consider the supplier-distributor relationship between airlines and retail travel agents. Long before airline deregulation, the relationship between the first airlines and travel agencies grew organically over time in response to consumer needs and the financial and technical satisfaction by these suppliers and intermediaries working with each other. The firms involved in the relationship meshed as complementary components that achieved a level of satisfaction for all firms involved. Over time these alliances evolved into a distribution system supported by the prompt payment of commissions in exchange for customers that supported and enhanced the relationship. Today, however, the need to cut costs and increase profits have led to most airlines reducing and capping commissions at levels where most travel agencies cannot sustain themselves. Though selling directly to the customer appears to be a sound financial strategy for airlines, one must wonder what the ultimate impact will be on the airlines who have created such adversarial conditions with travel agencies since choice is something consumers generally want more, not less, of and most will continue to prefer purchasing airline tickets through an intermediary. Great strategic advantages can be obtained by airlines who break ranks with the major airlines and seek closer cooperative relationships with retail travel agents.

Today, alliances are instrumental to a corporate strategy (Kotler, Bowen and Maken 1998), but most are not entered into nor maintained with careful thought. Many reflect a "ready-fire-aim" approach to relationship development where firms create alliances to meet strategic goals without implementing the appropriate mechanisms to assure relationship survival. In addition, we see examples of short-term power imbalances where one firm exerts power over another that undermines trust and threatens the dissolution of the alliance.

To achieve world class competitive levels a firm must increase its effectiveness to reach, serve and satisfy its target markets, while at the same time lower costs. Leading firms have found that one cannot achieve the twin goals by going-it-alone. Large conglomerates seldom are sustainable over time as evidenced by the break-up of American Express in the 1980s and the downsizing of JAL in the late 1990s. Through alliances, firms can gain market dominance and global reach that are beyond the resources of one firm to create and sustain alone.

CREATING A PARTNERSHIP

There are five critical questions that need to be addressed before creating a partnership. They are:

1. Do we want to partner?
2. Do we have an ability to partner?
3. With whom do we partner?
4. How do we partner?
5. How do we sustain and renew a partnership over time?

Do We Want to Partner?

In answering the first question one needs to assess the degree to which partnering can play a role in helping the firm obtain strategic advantages in the marketplace. Strategic advantage is derived from a partnership where a joint action can achieve something the customer will value at a reduced risk for all firms involved. Technological innovations, increased service and market coverage at less costs appear to be the reasons why many travel and tourism firms agree to partner. However, partnering is often a competitive response because others in the industry are gaining strategic advantages through their own partnerships and the other firms feel compelled to counter with alliances of their own.

Do We Have an Ability to Partner?

To be a good partner one must be ready to partner. Being a good partner often requires a cultural change in an organization and its people. This question requires that a firm perform an internal audit of its own ability to be a good partner. Reputation, performance capabilities, win-win orientation and the ability to create and sustain trust is central to attracting the right partner. Often we find firms that have a difficult time working collaboratively within their own organization, let alone with an outside firm. Individuals need to understand why external alliances are important, how to support the external relationship, and be evaluated and rewarded accordingly.

With Whom Do We Partner?

The first step in selecting a partner is to select the areas where a potential partner will have a positive impact on one's business. Wilson (1996) provides two methods useful for categorizing potential partners. In Figure 1, the potential value of a partner (vertical axis) is accessed on a multi-dimensional scale including such items as impact on profits, market penetration, market coverage and technological innovations. Each firm must develop its own set of measures with which to define a partner's potential value. The horizontal axis is the ability to partner with the other firm. Ability to partner is the flip-side of the previous question in that one should evaluate the ability of the other firm to partner successfully. Low cultural fit, lack of trust and poor communication can all be impediments to achieving a successful relationship. Firms in the upper right hand quadrant are both important to a firm's long term success and possess a high ability to partner successfully. The more difficult situation is exhibited by those firms in the quadrant that are high in importance but have a low ability to partner. Here a firm needs to ascertain if one can overcome

FIGURE 1. Partner Selection Criteria

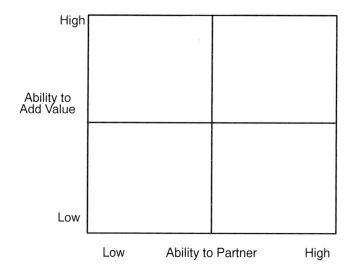

the root causes of its counterpart's low ability to partner. In some instances it may be impossible to overcome these differences.

Another more market oriented method of sorting potential partners purported by Wilson (1996) is described in Figure 2. The ability to add value addresses the issue previously discussed on building strategic advantage. In assessing a potential partner's ability to lower your firm's operating risk, one should consider such items as consistent high quality, reliable performance and trust in the other firm not to act opportunistically.

How Do We Partner?

A number of scholars have developed reasonably well-supported models of successful buyer-seller alliances (Dwyer, Schurr and Oh 1987, Heide and George 1990, Morgan and Hunt 1994, Crotts and Wilson 1995, Wilson 1996). Although they vary in specific details, they all use similar constructs that influence the success or failure in a relationship. Johanson, Lars and Nazeem's (1991) definition of a relationship is useful in that it applies the elements of these conceptual models. For Johanson et al. "a strategic alliance is defined as an inter-organizational relationship where the partners make substantial investments in time, effort and resources in developing long-term collaborative effort and common orientation towards meeting individual and mutual goals." Inherent in this definition and operationalized in nearly all the success models of relationship development are:

- Reputation
- Performance Capabilities
- Goal Compatibility
- Trust
- Strategic Advantage
- Amount of Adaptations/Non-Retrievable Investments
- Communication
- Cooperation
- Social Bonding

For reasons of parsimony, the reader is referred to Crotts and Wilson (1995) or Crotts, Aziz and Raschid (1998) for operational definitions of each of these constructs. The point is that these are variables that must be successfully communicated or evoked in order to attract and retain the interest of a prospective partner in a joint alliance.

How Does a Partnership Sustain and Renew Itself over Time?

The Chinese symbol for crisis is the combination of two characters. One character depicts danger and the other depicts opportunity. This is a perfect description of our current understanding of relationship development. Great opportunities exist for firms that form strong synergistic alliances to grow and flourish. At the same time there is great danger if the relationship fails as a firm can loose competitive position as well as a great deal of money.

FIGURE 2. Evaluating the Value of a Potential Partner

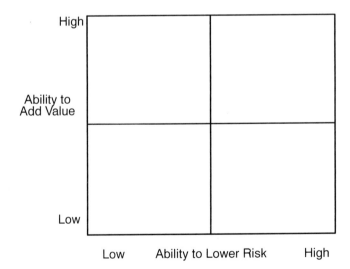

The danger in alliances (Han, Wilson and Dant 1993) as perceived by business persons seems to be the fear of becoming overly dependent upon the partner and a fear of opportunity loss because one partner may not provide you an innovation in the future that another firm can. Firms also have a major concern about sharing data which can create power imbalances that can be used against them in future negotiations. There is also a fear of losing the ability to act independently as they become more intricately meshed in a partnership. Many of these fears can be justified if a firm has not carefully developed their partnering skills outlined previously.

Though the future is unclear, we can be sure that alliances and strategic partnering will be in the future for the travel and tourism industry. To meet the future, firms should develop programs for partnering that will facilitate the necessary cultural and operating changes necessary to build successful and durable alliances and partnerships.

SELECTED APPLICATIONS
OF STRATEGIC ALLIANCE RESEARCH

Alliances, relationships and strategic partnerships manifest themselves in many forms. As it is impossible to describe all areas of relationship research that are relevant to hospitality and tourism, this collection will be limited to a number of areas. The following discussion briefly describes the seven research articles contained in this special volume. Collectively they describe relationships between (a) buyers-sellers; (b) suppliers-distributors; and (c) multiple suppliers in various collaborative efforts. In addition, an article is included that focuses on the cooperative relationship between management and employees in a multi-ethnic business environment. All the studies provide insights as to the factors that influence the formation and stabilization of alliances as well as the theoretical contexts in which they can be viewed. Hopefully, this special collection will generate further a dialog on the creation and management of alliances as well as invite further research in an area largely neglected by hospitality and tourism researchers.

Inbound tour operators perform an important role as travel intermediaries that link local tourism suppliers with overseas wholesalers and outbound agents. March (this issue) explores how inbound operators, acting as buyers on behalf of overseas clients, make purchase decisions for three types of suppliers–hotels, restaurants, and coach companies. The relationship marketing implication for suppliers suggests that tourism operators need to develop differentiated marketing strategies depending on the inbound tourism market they are targeting.

Tourism by its very nature has had a long history of inter-cultural exchanges. Increased international travel and the desire of firms to expand internationally creates circumstances that bring together individuals and firms from different national cultures under a collaborative effort. Such an environment raises interesting research questions as to how and to what degree national culture influences the relationship development process.

Money (this issue) explores the issue of whether national culture and location influences the way corporate purchasing managers find and select their corporate travel agent of choice. Framed under Social Networks Theory, Japanese companies whether operating in Japan or the U.S. made more use of referral networks than American companies. On the other hand, U.S. companies operating in Japan did not appear to conform their purchasing habits to the norms of the host culture. In an intra-firm setting, Waser and Johns (this issue) examine the influence of different cultural ethnicities of hotel workers and managers upon the team culture of workgroups. In their study of two large ethnically diverse five-star hotels in London, the source of worker discontent with management was more associated with inter-cultural misunderstandings than the task of delivering excellent customer service. Both of these studies reveal that creating functional relationships between individuals from different national cultures adds complexity in the relationship development process. Inter-cultural exchanges, be they business to business or employee to employee related, is an area largely neglected in hospitality and tourism research.

A number of case studies are presented in this volume to illustrate not only the importance but also the difficulties in developing and maintaining alliances. Telfer (this issue) shares insights gleaned from principals in an alliance of food producers, processors, wineries, distributors, hotels, restaurants and chefs in the "Taste of Niagara." The success of the alliance in bringing together these parties under a regional tourism brand if successful will pay dividends not only to the region's tourism interests but to the small farms in the vicinity.

Fyall, Oakley and Weiss (this issue) provide insights on the origin, development and collaborative dynamics of an alliance designed to promote the inland waterways of Britain and Ireland to international markets. The chief architects of the alliance were the British Tourist Authority and the TMS Partnership. The alliance includes numerous public and private interests involved in environmental protection, economic development and the five largest hire-boat operators. The authors frame their discussion under a number of theoretical contexts in order to explain the differing degrees of participation among the partners in the collaborative effort.

Buhalis (this issue) explores the distribution channel of tourism and illustrates the power imbalances that exist between members. In particular he illustrates the problems that small hoteliers in the Greek islands face with powerful tour operators and illustrates a wide range of methods used in order to increase their bargaining power. As tour operators become much more integrated in the European context whilst information technologies continue to revolutionize the distribution channel, this chapter enables authors to appreciate the dynamic nature of distribution and the importance of relationships management.

The issue concludes with an article by Domke-Damonte (this issue) who tested the performance effects of airlines that form cooperative alliances with other industry counterparts. Basing her research upon an historical analysis (14 year period) of the U.S. domestic airline industry, her findings suggest that only under periods of environmental volatility do cooperative alliances improve airline profits. These results suggest that firms should be cautious in over-committing themselves to an excessive number of collaborative efforts, and thereby neglecting their competitive market position.

REFERENCES

Buhalis, Dimitrios (this issue). Relationships in the Distribution Channel of Tourism: Conflicts Between Hoteliers and Tour Operators in the Mediterranean Region. *International Journal of Hospitality & Tourism Administration, Vol. 1* (1).

Crotts, John C. , Aziz, Abdul and Raschid, Andrew (1998). Antecedents of supplier's commitment to wholesale buyers in the international travel trade. *Tourism Management, Vol. 19* (2), 127-134.

Crotts, John C. and Wilson, David T. (1995). An integrated model of buyer-seller relationships in the international travel trade. *Progress in Tourism and Hospitality Research, Vol. 1* (2), 125-139.

Domke-Damonte, Darla J. (this issue). The Effect of Cross-Industry Cooperation on Performance in the Airline Industry. *International Journal of Hospitality & Tourism Administration, Vol. 1* (1).

Dwyer, F. R., Schurr, P. and Oh, S. (1987). Developing Buyer-Seller Relationships. *Journal of Marketing, Vol. 51* (2), 11-27.

Fyall, Alan, Oakley, Ben and Weiss, Annette (this issue). Theoretical Perspectives Applied to Inter-Organisational Collaboration on Britain's Inland Waterways. *International Journal of Hospitality & Tourism Administration, Vol. 1* (1).

Han, Sang-Lin, Wilson, David T. and Dant, Shirish (1993). Buyer-Seller Relationships Today. *Industrial Marketing Management*, Vol. 22 (4), 331-38.

Heide, J. and George, J. (1990). Alliances in Industrial Purchasing: The Determinants of Joint Action in Buyer-Seller Relationships. *Journal of Marketing Research, Vol. 27* (1), 24-36.

Johanson, J., Lars, H. and Nazeem, S.M. (1991). Interfirm adaptation in business relationships. *Journal of Marketing, Vol. 55* (2), 29-37.

Kotler, J., Bowen, J. and Maken, J. (1998). *Marketing for Hospitality and Tourism.* Upper Saddle River, N.J.: Prentice Hall.

March, Roger (this issue). Buyer Decision-Making Behavior in International Tourism Channels. *International Journal of Hospitality & Tourism Administration, Vol. 1* (1).

Morgan, Robert, and Hunt, Shelby (1994). The commitment-trust theory of relationship marketing. *Journal of Marketing, Vol. 58* (2), 20-38.

Money, R. Bruce (this issue). Social Networks and Referrals in International Organizational Buying of Travel Services: The Role of Culture and Location. *International Journal of Hospitality & Tourism Administration, Vol. 1* (1).

Telfer, David J. (this issue). Taste of Niagara: Building Strategic Alliances Between Tourism and Agriculture. *International Journal of Hospitality & Tourism Administration, Vol. 1* (1).

Waser, Helmut and Johns, Nick (this issue). Team Needs and Management of Multi-Ethnic Workgroups in Hotels. *International Journal of Hospitality & Tourism Administration, Vol. 1* (1).

Wilson, David T. (1996). An Integrated Model of Buyer-Seller Relationships. *Journal of the Academy of Marketing Science, Vol. 23* (4), 335-345.

Buyer Decision-Making Behavior in International Tourism Channels

Roger March

SUMMARY. Despite the development and maintenance of effective channel relationships in international tourism markets being critical to a firm's success, little research has been undertaken in business-to-business relationships in cross-national markets (March 1997a; Crotts, Aziz & Raschid 1998). This research paper offers insights into the decision-making behavior of a critical intermediary in international tourism channels, the inbound tour operator (ITO). In an exploratory study, the purchasing attitudes of ITOs, in their functions as purchasers of tourism products on behalf of overseas clients, are examined. Respondents were asked to assess the importance of a number of supplier attributes for three types of tourism products: hotels, coach companies and restaurants. Twenty-six inbound tour operators specialising in the Asian or Japanese inbound markets into Australia were surveyed; though small in number these firms handled over 800,000 visitors to Australia in 1998 (including 82% of the entire Japanese market). The results from a 43-item questionnaire, designed after preliminary discussions with ITOs, reveal differences between the attitudes of Japanese-market and Asian-market ITOs in their purchase decision-making behavior and in buyer attitudes toward different product types. The findings offer useful lessons for suppliers in the management of their relationships with inbound tour operators. *[Article copies available for a fee from The Haworth Document Delivery Service: 1-800-342-9678. E-mail address: getinfo@haworthpressinc.com <Website: http://www.haworthpressinc.com>]*

Roger March is affiliated with the School of Marketing, University of New South Wales, Sydney 2052 Australia (e-mail: r.march@unsw.edu.au).

The author would like to thank colleague and friend Michael Edwardson for his invaluable assistance.

[Haworth co-indexing entry note]: "Buyer Decision-Making Behavior in International Tourism Channels." March, Roger. Co-published simultaneously in *International Journal of Hospitality & Tourism Administration* (The Haworth Press, Inc.) Vol. 1, No. 1, 2000, pp. 11-25; and: *Global Alliances in Tourism and Hospitality Management* (ed: John C. Crotts, Dimitrios Buhalis, and Roger March) The Haworth Press, Inc., 2000, pp. 11-25. Single or multiple copies of this article are available for a fee from The Haworth Document Delivery Service [1-800-342-9678, 9:00 a.m. - 5:00 p.m. (EST). E-mail address: getinfo@haworthpressinc.com].

KEYWORDS. International tourism, distribution, business-to-business marketing, Japanese tourism, purchase decision-making, inbound tour operators

INTRODUCTION

Purchase decision making in business-to-business markets is often a complex and dynamic process (Bunn 1993). Patterns of customer buying behavior differ according to product, market and environment. While organizational buyer behavior has received significant research attention in the marketing literature over many years (see recent reviews by Kauffman 1996 and Bunn 1990 & 1993), there has been little investigation into buyer behavior in the service industry in general, and tourism in particular. Two exceptions in the tourism literature can be cited. Crotts, Aziz and Raschid (1998) examined the factors that shaped the seller's commitment to buyers in the context of the New Zealand travel trade. Similarly, buyer-supplier relationships in inbound tourism have been investigated from the perspective of supplier dependency in an olisopsonistic market (March 1997b).

The lack of research into cross-national aspects of international tourism is well documented (see, for example, Dimanche 1994; Pizam & Jeong 1996; Hu 1996; Crotts, Aziz and Raschid 1998). The marketing research that is undertaken in international tourism predominantly focuses on the tourist, and most of that is proprietary information generated by national tourism organizations. Trade marketing issues are rarely addressed. For example, a recent discussion of the role of research in tourism makes no mention of business-to-business research issues (Taylor 1996).

In business-to-business relationships, transactions are not ad hoc decisions but occur in the context of on-going relationships among the parties concerned. It has been argued that "the firm's activities in industrial markets are cumulative processes in the sense that relationships all the time are established, maintained, developed, and broken in order to give satisfactory, short-term economic return. . . ." (Johanson & Mattsson 1987, p. 45). In the case of inbound tourism from Asia and Japan into Australia this is a particularly relevant since personal relationships are often cited by Australian tourism operators as critical to success in doing business with their overseas counterparts (March 1997a).

For suppliers, understanding the purchasing behavior of buyers is essential for effective management of their marketing efforts. In international tourism markets, the buying decision-making processes are complex due to the influences of distance and the number of decision makers in the channel. In the case of Japanese package travel to Australia, for instance, the selection of hotels for particular package product tours will be made by product planners in Tokyo, but the final booking will be made by an inbound tour operator in Australia.

While the policy of most Japanese wholesalers is to specify hotels in their more expensive package tours, for less expensive itineraries wholesalers will specify only the grade of hotel, leaving the final decision about which hotel is selected to the inbound tour operator. Regarding other tourism components, such as coach transport, attractions and restaurants, the inbound tour operator is often the sole decision maker. As we can see, therefore, the inbound tour operator plays a pivotal role in the purchasing decisions in inbound tourism.

Despite this importance, there has been little research and scant acknowledgement of the ITO in either the academic tourism literature or tourism marketing textbooks. For example, Morrison (1996) and Middleton (1994) use the term 'tour operator' to mean both inbound tour operators in the international market and coach operators who sell tours to the general public; Kotler, Bowen & Makens (1996), meanwhile, make no mention at all of tour operators. Perhaps the 'below-the-line' marketing activities of the ITO (see Figure 1) have hidden its key distribution function from the inquiring eyes of academic researchers.

The only other research undertaken with a similar marketing perspective is the Gymn and Jacobs (1990) study into the important decision variables considered by Japanese import managers when selecting overseas suppliers. Like the present study, the authors emphasized the relative importance of the decision variables among competing products. The findings, however, are not generalizable beyond the consumer market. (For example, the main problems associated with importing were quality control, lack of dependable suppliers, timely delivery and communication problems.)

RESEARCH SETTING

This research paper examines the purchasing attitudes of a key buyer in international tourism markets, namely, the inbound tour operator (ITO).

FIGURE 1. ITO Position in International Distribution Channel

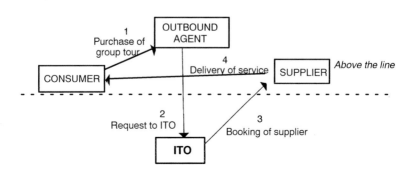

Known also by the term 'land operator,' the ITO arranges the itineraries and assembles the components of group tours on behalf of outbound travel agents located in overseas source markets. Outbound agents may be tour wholesalers, conference and incentive organizers, retail travel agents or travel companies who create group travel programs for sale to end-users (for example, arranging educational tours for high-school students or sporting tours for college students during summer vacations). The ITO does not come into contact with the traveller. Rather, the ITO provides the middle-man function by booking and paying tourism suppliers on behalf of their overseas client. (The exception is, in the case of the Australian tourism industry at least, where many inbound operators employ their own tour guides, rather than contract this critical tourism component to outside companies that may have less compunction to ensure the delivery of a quality service.)

Local tourism suppliers in Australia (as in most countries) rely on ITOs for a substantial amount of their inbound business. In immature yet emerging outbound travel markets, such as those found in several countries in Asia (e.g., Korea, Indonesia, Malaysia and Thailand) the ITO's role is particularly critical for two reasons: the relative inexperience of the Asian overseas traveller (leading to the preference for inclusive package tours) and the inexperience of the Asian outbound agent (who has little or no product knowledge of foreign destinations and few resources to commit to establishing a representative presence in those key destinations). It has been shown that the Asian wholesaler, especially, relies heavily on the experience and advice of the ITO with regard to choice of destination (within the country) as well as decisions about products, whether hotel, coach company or attraction (March 1997a). Even in a market as sophisticated as the Japanese, ITOs will handle the work of both large and small tour wholesalers (March 1997b).

For the purposes of this exploratory study, only ITOs specializing in the Asian and Japanese inbound markets, rather than all ITOs operating in Australia, were selected for investigation. This decision was made for two reasons. First, the Asian and Japanese markets are highly structured: package tours, together with other group travel such as incentives, account for a greater number of visitors than does FIT travel (BTR 1998). The structure of the market means that the overseas wholesaler plays a more dominant role than it does in Australia's other key inbound markets, such as North America, Europe and the United Kingdom (BTR 1998). Secondly, anecdotal evidence indicates that a fair degree of uncertainty exists in the minds of tourism suppliers operating in the Asian and Japanese markets about the purchasing priorities and needs of ITOs themselves, and ultimately, of the needs and expectations of the end-user, the inbound visitor. This research seeks to contribute to our understanding of the factors that influence ITO purchasing decisions for the three main tourism components of group tours–hotels, coach companies and restaurants.

SAMPLING AND DATA COLLECTION

The research was carried out in two stages. The first stage adopted an inductive, qualitative approach in order to identify the issues of importance to industry participants. A series of in-depth interviews were conducted with inbound tour operators to gain an understanding of the attributes they considered important when selecting tourism suppliers. The researcher interviewed managers responsible for purchasing in two of the largest Japanese-owned ITOs (specializing in the Japanese market) in Australia and two leading Asian ITOs; in addition, a highly respected tourism industry consultant was interviewed to obtain a third-party's perspective. The use of qualitative research at the preliminary stage was also necessitated by the lack of supporting research instruments in a similar research setting. This grounded theory approach works because "rather than forcing data within logico-deductively derived assumptions and categories, research should be used to generate grounded theory, which 'fits' and 'works' because it is derived from the concepts and categories used by social actors themselves to interpret and organise their worlds" (Jones 1987).

These interviews generated four main decision-making variables and a number of related statements (questionnaire items). The four main variables identified were: (1) financial and managerial issues (generating nine statements covering such issues as pricing and the supplier's management structure), (2) relationship issues (seven statements such as closeness of personal contacts in the supplier organization), (3) market knowledge (eight statements such as supplier's knowledge of distribution channels and of the appropriate target market(s) for its product), and (4) product quality and service delivery (nineteen statements ranging from supplier's reputation to whether the supplier employs foreign-speaking staff). In all, forty-three statements were generated.

During the interviews, the buyers stated that they evaluated different suppliers in different ways; for example, some factors were important when deciding among hotels, but these factors were far less important when considering other supplier types. It was therefore decided to incorporate into the questionnaire design the means by which respondents could individually evaluate their three main suppliers: hotels, coach companies and restaurants. These three products satisfy the basic needs of international tourists: shelter, food and transport. (Other suppliers, such as attractions, are less important because outbound agents require them only infrequently to be included in group tours; groups tourists are more likely to be offered attractions as optional tours after they arrive in the overseas destination.) A 7-point Likert scale, which asked respondents the extent to which they agreed or disagreed with each statement for each of the three product categories, was devised.

A pilot test followed, in which multiple respondents were asked to add important issues or to delete items they deemed unsuitable or inappropriate. This review procedure of the research instrument allowed testing for construct validity (Easterby-Smith, Thorpe, & Lowe 1991). The final questionnaire was then mailed to forty-five (45) purchasing managers and CEOs in Australia's main Asian and Japanese inbound tour companies (twenty-one (21) in the Japanese market and twenty-four (24) in the Asian market). Self-addressed, stamped envelopes were enclosed for the convenience of respondents. The sampling frame was generated from mailing lists obtained from the Inbound Tourism Organisation of Australia (ITOA) and two major Sydney-based tourism suppliers who deal extensively in the Asian and Japanese inbound markets. Based on industry interviews, the Japanese ITOs were expected to account for some 65% of the entire Japanese market into Australia, while the Asian ITO respondents were likely to account for some 30-40% of the Asian market.

The researcher contacted forty-percent of the respondents by telephone prior to them receiving the questionnaire and asked for their assistance in completing it. (Time and funding constraints prevented all respondents from being contacted before mailing. Also, it was deemed culturally inappropriate to have a young research assistant contact Asian CEOs, regardless of the size of their firms, and ask for their assistance.) Two weeks after mailing, the researcher personally contacted by telephone the firms that had not responded.

Of the surveys mailed out, 26 questionnaires were returned, for an effective response rate of 65%. (Of the original 45 sample, two firms had closed down, two replied that they were not involved in either market, and one return was lost in the mail.) Three ITOs handled markets in addition to Asia and/or Japan; in all these cases, Japan was a more important market than particular Asian countries and therefore they were included in the survey as Japanese market ITOs for convenience purposes. The break-up of Japanese to Asian ITOs was 14:12, representing a response rate of 70% and 65%, respectively. The response rates are consistent with those obtained in other distribution channel surveys (Murry & Heide 1998). Chart 1 shows the numbers of passengers handled by the ITOs surveyed (in percentage terms).

The main Asian markets served by the ITOs were Hong Kong (3 ITOs named this as their main market), followed by Singapore (2), Malaysia (1), Taiwan (1), and China (2). It should be noted that no ITOs specializing in the Korean market were included in the survey. While this country was Australia's fastest-growing inbound market prior to the outbreak of the Asian eco-

CHART 1. Passengers Handled by ITO Respondents (%)

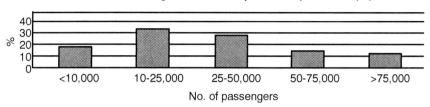

No. of passengers

nomic crisis in late 1997, the market has fallen 80% during 1998 (ABS Statistics 1998).

Respondents were also asked which travel segments they served in each market. (Again, these segments were created after consultation with the industry.) They were given the choice of FITs, incentive/conference groups, group tours, special interest tours (SITs), student/study groups, sporting tours, and honeymooners. For Japanese ITOs, the main segments were group travel, followed by FITs, incentive/conference groups and honeymooners. Asian ITOs usually handled several markets and quite often different travel segments in different markets. The average number of markets handled by Asian ITOs was 5.2, and the main travel segments were FITs and group tours.

RESULTS

The data were analyzed using SPSS Ver. 8.0. The results were examined along a number of dimensions: ranking of individual item importance, differences and similarities according to Japanese or Asian ITOs, and according to supplier category (hotel, coach or restaurant).

As explained earlier, the small sample generated was a function of the nature and structure of the tourism industry. Twenty-three respondents revealed the number of passengers they expected to handle during 1998. The passengers handled by the fourteen Japanese ITOs (all of whom revealed their figures, against three Asian ITOs who did not) totaled 603,000 or a remarkable 82% of *all* expected Japanese visitors to Australia during the year. (In fact, the top six ITOs handled 65% of all expected Japanese visitors.) In contrast, the nine Asian ITOs were responsible for 198,000 inbound Asian visitors, or 21% of the forecast arrivals in 1998 (forecasts sourced from Tourism Forecasting Council 1998). The heavy market concentration evident in the Japanese market reflects the oligopsonistic nature of this unique outbound market and makes the findings for this key market particularly meaningful for suppliers.

Table 1 lists the most important decision-making factors that ITOs consider when choosing from among the three supplier groups; while Table 2 lists

TABLE 1. Ten Main Decision-Making Factors

N = 26		Mean ranking	Mean	S.D.
1	The supplier has 100% public liability insurance.	6.60	5.99	1.09
2	The supplier operates 365 days a year.	6.49	5.89	1.31
3	Our company has had a long relationship with the supplier.	5.74	5.74	1.01
4	The supplier is prepared to lower its rates when we make reasonable requests.	5.72	5.52	1.43
5	There is always someone I can contact in the supplier organisation.	5.60	5.64	0.87
6	The supplier can guarantee its rates 12-18 months in advance.	5.37	5.41	1.23
7	The supplier always delivers what it promises.	5.18	5.36	1.37
8	The supplier can handle large groups.	4.87	5.38	1.09
9	We have good personal contacts in the supplier organisation.	4.81	5.28	1.35
10	The supplier has excellent reputation.	4.63	5.23	1.40

TABLE 2. Ten Least Important Decision-Making Factors

N = 26		Mean ranking	Mean	S.D.
34	The supplier can satisfy the special needs of ethnic/cultural groups.	6.18	4.60	1.06
35	The supplier has the best location.	6.17	4.52	1.14
36	The supplier employs foreign-speaking guides/front-line staff.	5.87	4.45	1.08
37	The supplier is not well served by a product similar to that offered by the supplier.	5.82	4.42	0.81
38	The product has been specifically designed for the inbound market.	5.72	4.53	1.18
39	The supplier has won numerous tourism awards.	5.67	4.32	1.04
40	The supplier offers the lowest rate.	5.60	4.29	1.67
41	The supplier provides foreign-language information.	5.56	4.36	1.21
42	Supplier understands our internal structure.	5.53	4.28	1.39
43	Senior management are Asian or Japanese.	2.88	3.23	1.12

the ten least important. Utilizing Friedman's non-parametric test, significant differences were identified in the way respondents ranked the items (p < .001). (For the ten most important factors, chi-square = 43.86, p < .001; for the ten least important chi-square = 85.33, p < .001).

Differences According to Supplier Type

Different variables were identified in terms of importance with regard to product type. These are shown in Table 3. Of the six categories in Table 3, the Least Important Factors for each product type was found to have a significant difference (p < .05). The reasons underlying the lack of significant differences in the other categories could be investigated in future research.

Differences Between Japanese and Asian ITOs

Utilizing Friedman's non-parametric test, the mean rankings for the Japanese ITOs and Asian ITOs are shown in Table 4 and Table 5, respectively. (For the Japanese buyers' ten main factors, chi-square = 122.61, p < .001; for the Asian buyers' ten main factors chi-square = 44.96, p < .001). Whilst the

TABLE 3. Decision-Making Factors, by Supplier Type

MOST IMPORTANT FACTORS	Mean	S.D.	LEAST IMPORTANT FACTORS	Mean	S.D.
Hotels			**Hotels**		
Supplier operates 365 days a year.	6.20	0.96	Senior management are Asian or Japanese.	3.20	0.96
Supplier has 100% public liability insurance.	6.08	1.04	Supplier offers the lowest rate.	4.32	1.78
We have a long relationship with the supplier.	5.84	1.03	Supplier understands our internal structure	4.44	1.08
Coach companies			**Coach companies**		
Supplier has 100% public liability insurance.	6.20	1.04	Senior management are Asian or Japanese.	3.08	0.95
We have a long relationship with the supplier.	6.04	0.79	Supplier provides foreign-language information.	4.04	1.24
Supplier operates 365 days a year.	6.00	1.26	Supplier has the best location.	4.20	1.22
Restaurants			**Restaurants**		
Supplier has 100% public liability insurance.	5.72	1.24	Senior management are Asian or Japanese.	3.36	1.41
Supplier operates 365 days a year.	5.60	1.66	Supplier understands our internal structure.	4.04	1.57
There is always someone I can contact in the supplier organisation.	5.52	0.96	The market is not well served by a product similar to that offered by the supplier.	4.28	0.84

TABLE 4. Japanese Market: Ten Most Important Factors

N = 26		Mean ranking	Mean	S.D.
1	The supplier has 100% public liability insurance.	7.13	6.03	0.99
2	The supplier operates 365 days a year.	6.96	5.53	1.53
3	There is always someone I can contact in the supplier organisation.	6.23	5.23	1.07
4	Our company has had a long relationship with the supplier.	6.21	5.70	0.92
5	The supplier can handle large groups (50+).	5.47	5.77	0.86
6	We have good personal contacts in the supplier organisation.	5.36	5.20	1.30
7	Supplier understands the inbound market well.	4.97	5.03	1.47
8	Supplier offers free site inspections when new products are introduced.	4.76	5.07	1.31
9	Supplier has long experience in the inbound market.	4.18	5.26	0.58
10	The supplier is used extensively by our competitors.	3.72	5.47	0.78

TABLE 5. Asian Market: Ten Most Important Factors

N = 26		Mean ranking	Mean	S.D.
1	The supplier has 100% public liability insurance.	6.58	6.07	1.03
2	The supplier operates 365 days a year.	6.35	6.11	1.12
3	The supplier is prepared to lower its rate when we make reasonable requests.	5.83	6.04	1.37
4	Our company has had a long relationship with the supplier.	5.76	6.11	0.89
5	There is always someone I can contact in the supplier organisation.	5.64	5.93	1.32
6	The supplier can guarantee rates 12-18 months in advance.	5.29	5.74	.944
7	The supplier does not reveal its rates to outbound agents.	5.22	5.89	1.05
8	The supplier always delivers what it promises.	5.19	5.96	1.12
9	Supplier has shown loyalty over the years.	4.64	5.78	1.08
10	The supplier's service quality is regarded as best in the industry.	4.50	5.74	.98

rankings of importance have been established for each market, it would be useful to know where the mean ratings for the factors differ between the two markets. For instance, only four factors are common to the ten most important attributes of both the Japanese and Asian markets: "The supplier has 100% public liability insurance," "Our company has long experience with the supplier," "The supplier operates 365 days a year," and "There is always someone in the organization I can contact." This could be explored in future research. Interestingly, the only variable that Japanese ITOs ranked significantly higher than their Asian counterparts was "The supplier is used extensively by our competitors." In the Asian market, this ranked the second least important consideration, while it ranked the fifth most important among Japanese.

Table 6 summarizes the results of the four cohorts developed conceptually. Due to the low sample size, factor analysis was inappropriate (Comrey 1973). In testing for reliability, Cochran's Alpha test revealed moderate and acceptable coefficients, as shown in the table. T-tests were used to test for significant differences between the means for the different cohorts between the two markets. There were significant differences between Asian and Japanese markets in the mean rating for Financial and Management Issues ($t = -2.57$, p < .01) and Relationship Issues ($t = -3.53$, p < .01). (Levene's test for non-homogeneity indicated that cohorts 1, 3 and 4 had unequal variances between markets; unequal t-values were used in the analysis.)

DISCUSSION

Qualitative versus Quantitative Results

Insights generated from the in-depth interviews differed somewhat from the results of the survey. Two issues dominated the minds of ITO managers interviewed: price and the lack of marketing expertise of many suppliers. Price appeared to be especially critical in the Asian market, in which ITOs were under pressure from Asian outbound agents to (often) seek the lowest price in the restaurant sector and low rates for hotels and coach transport. Though anecdotal evidence suggests that the Japanese market is a little more price inelastic, perhaps a consequence of the high product standards demanded by many Japanese travellers, ITOs in this market also complained of pressures from their clients to reduce prices, especially on hotels.

TABLE 6. Mean Scores of Cohorts

n = 26		Market	Mean	Std. Deviation	Alpha coefficients
1	Financial & management issues	Japanese	4.72	.96	0.73
		Asian	5.17	.45	
2	Relationship issues	Japanese	5.02	.81	0.74
		Asian	5.64	.74	
3	Market knowledge	Japanese	4.86	1.01	0.86
		Asian	4.94	.76	
4	Product quality & service delivery	Japanese	4.91	.70	0.85
		Asian	4.93	.49	

The lack of marketing expertise involved two issues: the inability of individual suppliers (regardless of category) to understand which particular inbound markets their products were suited for, and the lack of knowledge about channels of distribution in international tourism. Let us consider the first issue. The inbound travel market is very complex. The 'market' is not a collection of homogeneous markets differentiated by country of origin. Each country is composed of numerous customer segments, with different spending patterns and different travel needs. The term 'Japanese market,' for example, was once suggestive of camera-toting, big-spending tourists. That is no longer true. While some consumer segments, most noticeably the honeymooners, still spend heavily on souvenirs and prefer to stay in 5-star accommodation (JTB Report '98), the dominant trend of recent years has been the rise of travellers seeking cheaper holidays with little or no inclusive components in their package tours. This divergence of customer needs in the Japanese market has created demand for 3-star accommodation and cheaper coach transport. Despite these changes, ITOs complained that too many suppliers lacked sufficient understanding about the differentiated customer segments of particular source markets.

The second criticism of suppliers concerned the perceived lack of understanding of distribution channels in inbound tourism. A particular concern was the tendency of some suppliers to reveal their net rates to outbound agents when the supplier made sales calls overseas. Such 'transparency' of rates by suppliers prevented the ITO from adding on its margin when quoting on travel components to those outbound agents. According to ITOs and many experienced suppliers, such sales methods by suppliers reflected their ignorance of distribution channels and their lack of awareness of the critically important role that ITOs play in the inbound industry.

Asian and Japanese Purchasing Priorities Differ

Wholesalers and other outbound agents in the Japanese outbound travel industry have considerable experience in outbound travel compared to their counterparts in leading Asian markets such as Taiwan, Malaysia, Korea and Hong Kong. Moreover, the needs and expectations of Asian and Japanese tourists are likely to also differ, mainly because of the difference in experience of overseas travel. (For example, all restrictions were removed on outbound travel from Japan in 1964, compared to 1979 for Taiwan and 1989 for Korea.) For these reasons, therefore, it is likely that the attributes that ITOs in each market seek in their suppliers will differ.

Differences in the main decision-making variables between the Asian and Japanese ITOs were identified in Tables 4 and 5. One interesting finding was the relatively higher importance Japanese ITOs attributed to the statement: 'The supplier is used extensively by our competitors.' This is likely to reflect the 'follow-the-leader' strategy of many Japanese companies (not simply those in travel). Much decision-making in Japanese firms is conservative, manifesting itself in a cautious approach to entering into new relationships. If market leader JTB, for example, chooses to use a new supplier, its main competitors are highly likely to utilize the supplier as well.

The Role of Price as Purchase Determinant

The survey results indicate that price as a determinant of purchasing decisions appears to be relatively less important than the preliminary interviews with ITOs suggested. There are good reasons why this may be the case. Purchase decision-making is a complex matter and purchasing managers facing a highly competitive environment are under constant pressure to minimize costs to the firms. Price preoccupies their minds. However, when decisions are actually made about suppliers other variables such as relationships, product quality and ultimate customer satisfaction come to the fore. Nevertheless, as indicated in preliminary interviews, price does appear to be a greater concern in the Asian market (Japanese ITOs ranked 'Supplier offers the lowest rate' as the second least important consideration (No. 42), compared to their Asian counterparts who ranked it No. 23).

Importance of Relationships Confirmed

The research findings confirm the importance of creating and maintaining relationships in business-to-business, and particularly international, marketing. Relationships ranked highly regardless of product type and market. The importance of developing sound personal relationships in business dealings among and with both Asians and Japanese is well documented (Lasserre and Schütte 1995). For that reason, Australian suppliers could expect that sound personal relationships are considered important by Asian and Japanese ITOs.

Ignorance of Market as Entry Barrier

The preliminary interviews with ITOs revealed their concern about the lack of understanding possessed by many suppliers with regard to the inbound market. Yet the results from the quantitative research suggested that this issue was of relatively lesser importance. These considerations should, therefore, be regarded as market entry barriers rather than as decision-making variables. Presumably, most of the suppliers used by ITOs on a regular basis have significantly more market knowledge than others still attempting to enter the inbound market. It is incumbent on ITOs, therefore, to provide better education for suppliers. (In Australia, only a handful of ITOs actually run regular workshops for suppliers to learn about the needs of the inbound market.)

The Myth of Same-Culture Purchasing Preferences

An interesting finding was that both sets of buyers placed the nationality of a supplier's firm as the least important supplier attribute. In the Australian community, at least, there is a widely held belief that Japanese operators prefer dealing only with Japanese-owned tourism businesses. Our results expose the lack of credence in this argument (see Tables 4 and 5).

LIMITATIONS AND SUGGESTIONS FOR FUTURE RESEARCH

The present research is a useful exploratory study of an area of international tourism that is little understood. The strength of the research is its focus on particular buyer attitudes toward the three main product categories that ITOs consider when arranging itineraries on behalf of overseas clients. The implications and lessons for new and existing suppliers in these two markets are self-evident. The weaknesses of the project lie in its narrow scope. First, the sample population is small, making quantitative analysis difficult. Yet to a certain extent this was inevitable, especially given the highly concentrated Japanese market in which the top fourteen buyers accounted for over 80 percent of the Japanese visitation to Australia. Secondly, this research treated the Japanese market as homogeneous, despite it having, as shown, multiple and evolving consumer segments. ITOs were not asked to differentiate among tourism products based on whether the customer segment was a big-spending honeymoon tour group or a group of budget-minded university graduates on an overseas holiday before entering the workforce. If they had, the importance they placed on particular issues might well have been different. Thirdly, the situational changes that affect purchase decision making were not considered. Bunn (1993), for example, identified a number of situational characteristics: purchase importance, purchase task uncertainty, extensiveness of the choice set and buyer power. These could be explored in future studies.

Other questions need to be asked. What is the relationship between customer needs and outbound agent requirements? In a perfect consumer-driven tourism market, the product supplier is chosen on its ability to satisfy the needs of the overseas visitor. But what of young, trade-driven markets such as Korea, where the traveller has little experience and probably unrealistic expectations of overseas travel. Research that explores the growth of outbound markets–in the same way that Butler (1981) developed his destination life-cycle–would be intellectually challenging and managerially useful from the viewpoint of a national tourism organisation. The appropriate methodology may be cross-cultural longitudinal research that charts an outbound market's shift from a trade-dominated to a consumer-driven market structure.

In a similar vein, the structure of distribution channels in international markets is another important topic. Markets differ in a number of ways: in terms of outbound agent dominance, structural characteristics, cultural needs of consumers (e.g., Muslim requirements for food and prayer rituals) and experience of the traveller (Singaporeans are highly experienced while the emerging Chinese and some Taiwanese require inclusive group travel). All these factors influence the structure and membership of distribution channels. Future researchers into the function and influence of ITOs might consider the evolutionary process by which channels of distribution emerge in a newly emerging outbound market. China is the obvious case-study.

CONCLUSIONS

The inbound tour operator, like other intermediaries in the tourism industry, is under threat of being by-passed by travel consumers who are increasingly turning to the Internet to contact and book with local suppliers. Yet the importance of the inbound tour operator in the international tourism distribution channel is unlikely to be diminished for some time to come. Particularly for small tourism businesses, which lack the financial capacity or managerial or marketing expertise to operate independently in the international marketplace, the ITO plays the invaluable 'middle-man' role. The findings reported here highlight purchase decision-making issues that previously only suppliers with considerable experience in the international market would be aware of. It is to be hoped that this small project increases the practitioner's understanding of distribution in international tourism.

REFERENCES

Australian Bureau of Statistics (1998) *Monthly Visitor Arrivals: August*
Bunn, M.D. (1990) "Understanding organizational buying behavior: the challenge of the 1990s," *Review of Marketing*
Bunn, M.D. (1993) "Taxonomy of Buyer Decision Approaches," *Journal of Marketing*, 57 (January), 38-56.
Bureau of Tourism Research (1998) *International Visitors Survey*, BTR: Canberra.
Butler, R.W. (1981) "The concept of a tourist area cycle of evolution: implications for management of resources," *The Canadian Geographer*, 24, 8-12.
Comrey, A.L. (1973) *A First Course in Factor Analysis*, Academic Press: New York.
Crotts, J. C., Aziz, A., and Raschid, A. (1998) "Antecedents of supplier's commit-

ment to wholesaler buyers in the international travel trade," *Tourism Management*, 19, 2, 127-134.

Dimanche, F. (1994) "Cross-cultural tourism marketing research: an assessment and recommendations for future studies," *Journal of Travel & Tourism Marketing*, 6, 3-4, 123-134.

Easterby-Smith, M., Thorpe, R. & Lowe, A. (1991), *Management Research: An Introduction*, Sage Publications: London.

Gymn, K.I. and Jacobs, L.W. (1990) "Import Purchasing Decision Behavior: An empirical study of Japanese import managers," *International Marketing Review*, 10, 4, 4-14.

Hu, C. (1996) "Diverse developments in travel and tourism marketing: a thematic approach," *International Journal of Contemporary Hospitality Management*, 8, 7, 33-43.

Johanson, J. and Mattsson, L-G. (1987) "Interorganizational Relations in Industrial Systems–A Network Approach Compared with the Transaction Cost Approach," *International Studies of Management and Organization*, 8 (1), 34-48.

Jones, S. (1987) "Choosing action research: a rationale" in I. L. Mangham (ed.), *Organization Analysis and Development*, Chichester: Wiley.

JTB Foundation (1998) *Japan Report '98*, JTB: Tokyo

Kauffman, R.G. (1996) "Influences on industrial buyers' choice of products: effects of product application, product type, and buying environment," *International Journal of Purchasing and Materials Management*, 30 (Spring), 28-38.

Kotler, P., Bowen, J. & Makens, J. (1996) *Marketing for Hospitality and Tourism*, Prentice-Hall International, Inc.: New Jersey.

Lasserre, P. and Schütte, H. (1995), *Strategies for the Asia Pacific*, Macmillan Education Australia: Melbourne.

March, R. (1997a) "Diversity in Asian Outbound Tourism Industries: A Field Study of the Outbound Tourism Industries in Indonesia, Thailand, Taiwan, South Korea and Japan," *International Journal of Hospitality Management*, 16 (2) June, 231-238.

March, R. (1997b) "Exploratory Study of Buyer-Supplier Relationships in International Tourism: The Case of Japanese Wholesalers and Australian Suppliers," *Journal of Travel & Tourism Marketing*, 6, 1, April, 55-68.

Morrison, A.M. (1996) *Hospitality and Travel Marketing*, Delmar Publishers: New York.

Middleton, V.T.C. (1994) *Marketing in Travel and Tourism*, Butterworth-Heinemann: Oxford.

Murry, J.P. Jr and Heide, J.B. (1998) "Managing Promotion Program Participation within Manufacturer-Retailer Relationships," *Journal of Marketing*, 62 (January), 58-68.

Pizam, A. and Jeong, G-H. (1996) "Cross-cultural tourist behavior," *Tourism Management*, 17, 4, 277-286.

Taylor, G.D. (1996) "A New Direction," *Journal of Travel & Tourism Marketing*, 5, 3, 253-263.

Tourism Forecasting Council (1998) *Forecast*, June, Office of National Tourism (Government of Australia).

Social Networks and Referrals in International Organizational Buying of Travel Services: The Role of Culture and Location

R. Bruce Money

SUMMARY. Most channels for the marketing of services are very short–delivery is the product. In the corporate travel business, however, travel agent intermediaries are used to source what are often very large purchases of travel services. What is the role of word-of-mouth referrals in the process and how does it vary across national/cultural boundaries, in this case, Japan and the U.S.? With data collected from companies in both countries, social network analysis is applied to examine how companies go about sourcing their business travel services. Results indicate that culture has more impact than location (foreign vs. domestic) in the referral process. *[Article copies available for a fee from The Haworth Document Delivery Service: 1-800-342-9678. E-mail address: getinfo@haworthpressinc.com <Website: http://www.haworthpressinc.com>]*

KEYWORDS. Word-of-mouth referrals, social networks, U.S. and Japanese travel trade

Many leisure travelers choose destinations outside their country of residence, making the study of international travel purchases an important addition to the tourism marketing literature. Within the global travel industry, Japan, the world's second largest economy, is an important market to un-

---

R. Bruce Money, PhD, is affiliated with the International Business Program Area, University of South Carolina.

[Haworth co-indexing entry note]: "Social Networks and Referrals in International Organizational Buying of Travel Services: The Role of Culture and Location." Money, R. Bruce. Co-published simultaneously in *International Journal of Hospitality & Tourism Administration* (The Haworth Press, Inc.) Vol. 1, No. 1, 2000, pp. 27-48; and: *Global Alliances in Tourism and Hospitality Management* (ed: John C. Crotts, Dimitrios Buhalis, and Roger March) The Haworth Press, Inc., 2000, pp. 27-48. Single or multiple copies of this article are available for a fee from The Haworth Document Delivery Service [1-800-342-9678, 9:00 a.m. - 5:00 p.m. (EST). E-mail address: getinfo@haworthpressinc.com].

derstand. A huge target for travel marketers, it perennially tops the list of overseas arrivals to the United States; in 1997, nearly the same number of Japanese visited the U.S. (5.4 million) as did Germans (2 million) and the British (3.7 million) combined (*Tourism Industries* 1998). This represents a 3.6% increase over 1996, despite Japan's gloomy economic climate. However, perhaps because of the recession, the competitive nature of the complex travel business in Japan has changed. More buyers are making arrangements on their own (Sullivan 1995), and tourism conglomerates are decreasing in size. Also, opportunities for non-Japanese firms to do business there seem to be on the rise because of the changes brought on by the collapse of the "bubble economy" (Johansson and Hirano 1996). In addition, the marked differences in culture and business practices between the U.S. and Japan (Ouchi 1981; Pascale and Athos 1981), make a cross-national comparison of the two travel markets interesting for theoretical reasons. The U.S. and Japan are therefore the subject countries of this study because they represent two important travel markets for practitioners as well as useful theoretical contrasts for academics.

Although most travel research is done at the retail or consumer level, this paper answers the call for more business-to-business travel research (Crotts and Wilson 1995), particularly in an international context (March 1997; Money and Crotts 2000). Although statistics cited above are for all arrivals (business and leisure), no doubt the Japanese, with their export-oriented, island-nation economy, do a great deal of traveling for both business and vacation purposes. The purpose of this paper is to explore how business travel services are sourced by businesses in Japan and the U.S. The study fits with the work of Kotler et al. (1998), who model the environmental, organizational, interpersonal, and individual factors that impact the behavior of business-to-business purchasers of travel services. The paper extends their model by adding two international dimensions: national culture and location of operation (foreign or domestic). In particular, it uses social network theory to examine how purchasers in two countries use word-of-mouth (hereafter WOM) referrals to find their travel agent of choice. The research questions addressed herein include: Does national culture (in this case Japanese or American) affect the way business customers use referral sources in finding and choosing a travel agent? Also, does location of the company relative to its culture of origin (foreign or domestic) make a difference in the process?

The paper is organized as follows: the conceptual background of the antecedents, national culture and relative location are explored in the context of WOM referrals in business-to-business service marketing. Hypotheses are forwarded and a study is described whereby 48 companies in the U.S. and Japan were interviewed to collect data to test the hypotheses. Results are presented and analyzed, with implications for academics and practitioners discussed.

THEORETICAL BACKGROUND AND HYPOTHESES

The conceptual model for the current research is presented in Figure 1. Much of the theoretical basis as well as the call for more Japan-related travel research is presented in Money and Crotts (2000). The current research proposes that national culture and relative location of operation both influence the social network activity of the buyer's referral process: how many sources the buyer consults, what are the nature of the ties with those referral sources ("tie strength"), and how strategically are the sources placed in the referral network ("centrality").

Word-of-Mouth Referrals in Business-to-Business Service Purchases

The theoretical model is set in the context of industrial (business-to-business) service purchases, in particular commercial purchases of travel services, where WOM has been shown to very persuasive (Crotts 1999). Many studies have examined the pervasive effect of WOM on the purchase process of a variety of products and services (Mahajan et al. 1990; Yale 1989). WOM has more of an influence on the diffusion of innovations than the innovativeness of the product itself (Sultan et al., 1990). The value of being first-to-market is significantly enhanced by social positive WOM (Horsky and Mate

FIGURE 1. Conceptual Model

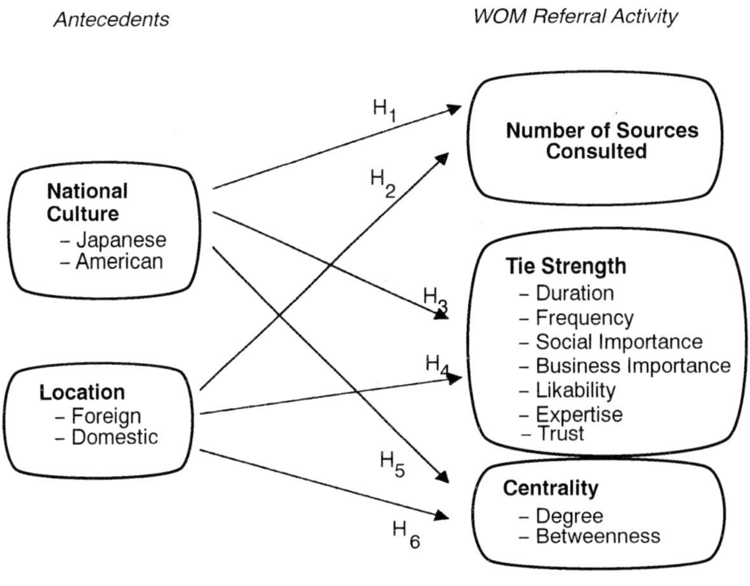

1988). WOM is seven times more effective than print advertising and four times more effective than personal selling convincing a customer to switch brands (Katz and Lazarsfeld 1955).

WOM is a critical component in measuring a consumer's susceptibility to interpersonal influence (Bearden et al., 1989). To service marketers, referrals have been shown to be all the more important (Berry and Parasuramen 1991; Haywood 1989), especially since informal channels of communication are the main channel of disseminating market information and many services are particularly complex and difficult to evaluate (File et al. 1992), such as professional services. WOM was shown to influence professional service expectations more than advertising, personal experience, or sales promotion (Webster 1991). Decisions regarding high involvement services such as medical care (Gelb and Johnson 1995; Webster 1988) and legal services (Crocker 1986) are especially subject to influence by referral sources–much as would professional travel services.

Almost all WOM studies have focused on consumer rather than organizational buying behavior. One organizational marketing study showed that a family business (compared to non-family) expects more prepurchase attention from industrial vendors, but rewards them with more positive WOM (File et al. 1994b). Business-to-business professional services literature that examines referral activity is fewer still (see File et al. 1994a), let alone any that focuses specifically on the travel industry, which obviously has a huge global presence. Kotler et al. (1998) dedicate a chapter to organizational buying behavior of travel services, but WOM is not addressed as a search mechanism. In attempting to fill the void, the current study proposes that various facets of WOM referral behavior are influenced by the study's two antecedent constructs: home-country culture (Japanese or American) and relative location (foreign or domestic).

National Culture: Japanese vs. American

National culture has been widely interpreted and utilized as an explanatory variable. Of the hundreds of definitions of national culture, Hofstede's (1991) "collective mental programming of the mind" is one of the most descriptive. Culture consists of patterns of behavior particular to a group of people, which patterns are learned, shared, and transmitted to the next generation. National culture has been used to study consumer behavior (Aaker and Maheswaran 1997; Penaloza 1994; Stayman and Deshpande 1989) as well as marketing executive decisions (Tse et al. 1988), explain global brand image strategies (Roth 1995), examine new product development (Nakata and Sivakumar 1996), and advance wider international marketing theory (Clark 1990). National culture has not generally been used to explain business-to-business buying behavior, in particular organizational travel purchases (Kotler et al. 1998), which void the current study seeks to fill.

Prominent amongst the operationalilzation of culture are the 5 dimensions of culture defined by Hofstede and his colleagues (Hofstede 1980, 1991) using the Value Survey Module, administered to 117,000 IBM employees in 53 countries. From the data in the IBM and other studies emerged the following dimensions and country scores for each, briefly defined:

1. *Individualism vs. collectivism:* a culture's emphasis on the identity of the individual person over that of the group. A "me" vs. "we" orientation.
2. *Uncertainty avoidance:* Tolerance for ambiguity, i.e., risk in life's experiences. Cultures low in uncertainty avoidance tend to emphasize stability, structure, and not taking risks.
3. *Masculinity vs. femininity:* A culture's achievement orientation vs. nurturing. Masculine cultures (not necessarily correlated with gender) emphasize competition; feminine cultures emphasize cooperation and collaboration.
4. *Power distance:* The degree to which social structure is formalized in a culture. Cultures low in this dimension are egalitarian, whereas high power distance cultures revere titles and social standing.
5. *Confucian dynamism:* Basically a long-term vs. short-term time horizon dimension. Given the Chinese root of the construct, cultures high in this dimension, such as most Asian cultures, emphasize long-range goals over short-term results.

Examining Hofstede's country scores for each dimension, probably the most explanatory for comparing the U.S. and Japan in the current study are individualism and uncertainty avoidance. The U.S. emerged as the most individualistic country in the world (Japan was near the mean) in Hofstede's data, while Japan scored the highest in uncertainty avoidance (the U.S. scored low). The Japanese penchant for risk-reducing group behavior in travel is manifest in the fact that most Japanese traveling abroad do so through travel conglomerates such as JAL and the Japan Travel Bureau, or JTB (Crotts and Wilson 1995); four out of five Japanese traveling abroad traditionally have done so under prepackaged tours (Japan Travel Bureau 1994).

Added to these dimensions of culture for the current study is the measure of *context* developed by Hall and Hall (1987). High context countries, such as Japan, Saudi Arabia, and China (Cateora and Graham 1998), use high degrees of innuendo, implicit code, and inference to convey meaning. A message's sender, timing, and situation may carry more meaning than the actual words themselves. On the other hand, low context cultures, such as Germany and U.S., value a "what you see is what you get" approach to communication, where candor, frankness, and detailed information are valued and encouraged (Tse et al. 1994). Higher context cultures tend to communicate more verbally, which behavior might lend itself to more WOM activity.

These cultural characteristics manifest themselves in a wide variety of business practices differences between the U.S. and Japan: The Japanese emphasize long-term growth and stability over market share (Anterasian et al. 1996), conduct business with common keiretsu (such as Mitsui or Sumitomo) industrial group companies before giving business to outsiders (Czinkota and Woronoff 1986), and spend six times the amount of per capita GNP as Americans on business entertainment (Sakaiya 1993) to develop proper context in business relationships. In the current study, Japanese companies are generally expected to engage in more intense social network WOM activity and use referral sources that are more collectivist and higher context in nature than Americans.

Location of Operation: Foreign vs. Domestic

In addition to a main effect for national culture, the current research examines the effect of relative location. That is, will the influence of national culture vary between situations where companies operate in environments of their home culture versus a foreign culture? Assuming that Japanese buyers behave exactly the same both inside and outside of Japan would be a mistake. For example, acculturation theory examines the results of two different cultures coming in direct contact with one another and how patterns in both groups change (Beals 1953). In the current study, acculturation theory would generate the following questions: Will purchasers of travel services take their business culture and practices with them when setting up a company in a foreign location? Or, is there something about the business environment in the foreign country that forces the new entrant to behave like others in that country? Previous literature has shown that a company's behavior in a foreign country is determined by two factors: its home culture and the culture of the foreign country (Tse et al. 1988). The current research theorizes that a company's WOM activity in a foreign market would differ from the pattern in its home-country culture because the company would tend to use informed intermediaries to locate the services that it uses. Such is consistent with research in cognitive psychology, which has shown that unfamiliar situations require two types of knowledge (Anderson 1983): procedural knowledge (how to), and contextual knowledge (relationships). In addition, March and Simon's (1958) bounded rationality concept asserts that organizations begin with the known to proceed to the unknown. A trusted intermediary (known) in a foreign market (unknown) would fit such a description. Finally, transaction cost analysis (Williamson 1975) infers that firms will seek to reduce their expense of either buying or building expertise in a foreign market. A company representative who asks key market informants for their help in forming business ties is an example of trying to keep transaction costs low. Hence, regardless of their culture, the current study hypothesizes that both Japanese and American companies in foreign markets will exhibit a greater degree of WOM referral seeking for their travel services.

Constructs and Measures from Social Networks Theory

Granovetter's (1973) research on the "strength of weak ties" was some of the first to consider how the characteristics of a relationship impact communication patterns in social networks. The term "network" in the current study refers to the patterns of social business interaction that arise in relationships between individuals who work for companies. In addition to Granovetter's tie strength concept, the current research also considers the number of referral sources used, and centrality, or how strategically a particular referral source is placed in a network. Although the concept has been used in several marketing and management studies (e.g., Money et al. 1998; Carroll and Teo 1996), very few researchers have considered networks of any kind in an international context (for an exception, see Ruan et al. 1997). Furthermore, studies of non-U.S. marketing relationships have been focused within a single country (Kale 1986, Frazier et al. 1989), unlike the cross-national context of the current research.

Number of WOM Referral Sources Consulted

Referral sources have been utilized as a dependent construct in several marketing studies in contexts ranging from piano tuners and teachers (Reingen and Kernan 1986; Brown and Reingen 1987) and home sales parties (Frenzen and Nakamoto 1993). In regards to the difference between WOM in Japan and the U.S., Takada and Jain (1991) found that innovation adoption rates were higher among Japanese and other Pacific Rim countries, who use more WOM than do Americans. Collectivist, risk avoidant, high context business-to-business relationships in Japan engender high levels of interpersonal trust (Sullivan and Peterson 1988), formed by more face-to-face meetings (Dyer and Ouchi 1993), where participants engage in "non-task sounding" (Graham and Sano 1989) and extensive business entertainment (Hall and Hall 1987). The Japanese may also use more WOM because of the difficulty of written communications in their character-based writing system (Pascale 1978). These differences are expected to manifest themselves in a higher number of referral sources contacted per search. Thus, the present research first hypothesizes that Japanese companies will employ more WOM referral sources to find sellers of commercial travel services than American companies, whether the companies are operating in Japan or the United States.

H_1:   Japanese buyers of commercial travel services will consult more WOM referral sources than American buyers.

In addition to national culture, relative location of operation (foreign vs. domestic) is also proposed to have an effect on the number of WOM sources consulted. Foreign buyers (Japanese in the U.S. and Americans in Japan) are hypothesized to use referral sources more than buyers operating in their home cultures or domestic markets (Japanese in Japan and Americans in the U.S.). Researchers have advised foreign marketers in Japan to work with a contact in an existing distribution channel (Nairu and Flath 1993), or consult an expert to lower transaction costs (Williamson 1975) in the target industry (Batzer and Laumer 1989). Personnel sent by headquarters to establish an office do better if they find a key informant to help (Gronhaug and Graham 1987). The discussion of procedural and contextual knowledge is pertinent here (Anderson 1983), as is the concept bounded rationality (March and Simon 1958) discussed above. Buyers in a foreign culture will seek out referral sources more than they would in their own markets:

H_2:   Buyers of commercial travel services in foreign markets will use more WOM referral sources than will buyers in domestic markets.

Tie Strength

Tie strength basically refers to the quality of the relationship between contacts. It has been used mostly in a consumer behavior setting to study issues such as brand congruence, that is, network contacts preferring similar brands (Reingen et al. 1984).

Prior research has also shown the strength of ties in subgroups and entire groups influences the likelihood that the tie will be activated (Reingen and Kernan 1986; Brown and Reingen 1987; Frenzen and Davis 1990). The measures of tie strength that have been employed in these studies are: *duration:* How long the seeker of the WOM referral and the source have known each other (Ward and Reingen 1990); *frequency of contact:* How often (instances per year, for example) the referral source and seeker of information contact each other (Brown and Reingen 1987); and *social importance:* How "important" the seeker considers the referral source (Reingen et al. 1984, Brown and Reingen 1987, Frenzen and Nakamoto 1993). To these we add four more measures related to the social psychology literature (McGuire 1985) that might help in capturing the nature of tie strength in a business-to-business setting: business importance (which can be distinct from social importance), likability, trust, and perceived expertise. The current research posits that a higher context, risk-avoidant, more collectivist Japanese would develop and use stronger ties between members of referral networks than Americans would, whether in the U.S. or Japan.

H_3:   The ties between buyers and referral sources in referral networks used by Japanese buyers of commercial travel services will be stronger than ties in networks used by American buyers.

Relative location (foreign vs. home-culture) is also proposed to have an effect, as addressed in the discussion for H1 and H2. That is, Japanese and Americans both will seek to lower their risk of incurring significant transaction costs by using a relatively known contact in a foreign market, with whom the buyer has strong ties, rather than an unknown (such as a Yellow Pages listing):

H_4:   The ties between buyers and referral sources in referral networks used by buyers of commercial travel services in foreign markets will be stronger than ties in networks used by buyers in domestic markets.

Centrality

Centrality is a measure of the importance of the position of a referral source in a network, that is, peripheral versus more strategic in terms of power and information flow (Bavelas 1950; Freeman et al. 1980). The construct has three components, two of which are germane to the current research: *degree* (number of common ties in the network between actors); and *betweenness* (how importantly or strategically the ties are placed). The third (*closeness*) is considered to have less explanatory power compared to the first two and is excluded from the study.

At its core, the centrality concept is mathematics and sociology, but a few management studies have utilized the construct, such as Ibarra and Andrews (1993). In marketing, Ronchetto et al. (1989) showed that centrality of workers in an industrial buying group influenced purchase decisions, although Freeman and his colleagues (1980) originally defined centrality for individuals, not groups. Likewise, the current research uses the concept to examine commercial travel service purchases. In fact, new centrality methods have defined the concept for "graphs," or groups of individuals (White and Borgatti 1994), which is useful in studying WOM referrals of both retail and commercial buyers. Referral sources used by Japanese buyers are expected to have higher centrality because they are the key social ties upon whom buyers are more dependent for information than Americans (Pascale and Athos 1981). Japanese consensus decision making (Graham and Sano 1989) also echoes the centrality concept. Thus, referral sources (in the "graph" or total network sense) in Japanese networks will be connected to more common sources (degree) and will be located more directly on the path of information flow (betweenness):

H_5:   Referral networks used by commercial Japanese buyers of travel services will have higher levels of graph centrality (degree and betweenness) than will networks used by American buyers.

Also, as discussed for previous hypotheses, an effect of location is also theorized. The referral networks of firms operating in foreign markets (Japanese in the U.S. and American firms in Japan) will exhibit higher levels of graph centrality because of the more strategically placed intermediaries they use. Again, this could be caused by relying on a key informant in order to introduce certainty into an uncertain environment. Buyers would be following advice of an opinion leader with high centrality, similar to the phenomenon of Feick and Price's (1987) so-called "market maven," someone who influences purchases by the authority of his or her superior knowledge of or experience with commercial travel service providers (agents) in a foreign market.

H_6:   Referral networks used by buyers of commercial travel services in foreign markets will have higher levels of graph centrality than will networks used by buyers in home-culture markets.

METHODS

Design

Testing the hypotheses herein requires a 2X2 matrix of culture (Japanese and American) and location (foreign and home country), a quasi-experimental design (Cook and Campbell 1979), as shown in Figure 2. The data were collected by interviewing small and medium sized companies in Japan and the U.S. about how they went about buying their commercial travel services. Details of data collection are also contained in Money et al. (1998), who examined 10 commercial services, aggregated with the travel agent data herein. The current study extends their research by focusing exclusively on the data and results for business-to-business travel services.

Sample

From library reference sources (such as *Southern California Business Directory* and Japan Export Trade Organization directories), an equal number of the four types of companies in the Figure 2 design were selected to

FIGURE 2. Research Design

NATIONAL CULTURE

	Japanese	American
Foreign **LOCATION**	1. Japanese companies in U.S. (Nissan USA)	2. American companies in Japan (Ford Japan)
Domestic	3. Japanese companies in Japan (Toyota)	4. American companies in U.S. (Chrysler)

(company names given as examples only)

Independent variables:
    1. National culture of firm (Japanese vs. American)
    2. Location of company (foreign vs. domestic)

Dependent variables:
    1. Number of sources consulted
    2. Tie strength
    3. Levels of centrality

interview (Japanese companies in the U.S., American companies in Japan, Japanese companies in Japan, American companies in the U.S.). Nationality differences were controlled by interviewing only individuals of the same "nationality" of the company (i.e., Americans were interviewed in American companies in Japan, not Japanese employees). To increase the study's generalizability, buying companies were chosen from three broad types of industries: those in the business of durable goods, those in nondurables, and those in services. The industries were chosen by SIC codes generated by a random number electronic spreadsheet function. The SIC code that most closely matched that number was chosen, then categorized as one of the three types above (durables, nondurables, and services) until 4 companies in each type were selected. Thus the total number of companies interviewed was 48–4 cells (e.g., Japanese in the U.S.) with 3 types of industries (durables, etc.), with 4 companies in each industry. The number of responses sought from each interviewee multiplied by the 48 companies was deemed sufficient to test the hypotheses herein. To keep the expense of data collection to reasonable levels, companies were interviewed in the five-county (San Diego, Los Angeles, Riverside, Orange and San Bernardino) southern California and

Tokyo areas, which in their own right are major economies in huge metropolitan areas (populations of over 10 million each). However, caution should be exercised in generalizing from these regions to the rest of the country.

Data Collection and Control Variables

The companies to be interviewed in southern California were contacted by the researcher by letter, asking for their help in studying service marketing. In Tokyo, the American Chamber of Commerce in Japan was used to contact American companies and various trade associations were utilized to contact Japanese companies, who would otherwise generally not answer an unsolicited interview request without an introduction. Certain criteria were used to control for age and size: only companies 10 years old or younger and companies smaller than 150 employees or less than $200 million in revenue were included. This was done because the service purchases are examined at the point of company inception. Smaller, younger companies would be more able to provide an interview with a person who was intimately involved in the purchase decision, such as a partner or founder. Such a person was requested to be present in the interview. In older, more established companies, the decision maker who made the original purchase may have left the company or not remember the process. If companies did not meet the sampling criteria or were unwilling to provide an interview, another company within the chosen buyer category (furniture or women's clothing, for example) was selected until all 48 interview slots were filled.

The researcher then visited the companies and conducted the in-depth interviews of approximately 60 minutes each. Questions were asked as prompts (McCraken 1988) such as, "How did you go about finding your travel agent?" If a referral was used, more questions were asked to take measures of tie strength (e.g., "On a scale from 1 to 5, how much did you trust this person?") and centrality ("Did this referral source refer you to any other services?") The interviews were conducted either in Japanese or English, depending on the subjects' preference, since the author is business fluent in both languages. The interviews in Japanese were tape recorded with the subjects' permission to ensure accurate translation of responses; copious field notes were taken in interviews conducted in English, the author's first language.

Measures

Number of sources consulted has one indicator, the total number of people (other than the seller itself) the buyer consulted in searching for the travel agent. Tie strength has 7 indicators, each measured on a 1 to 5 Likert scale. Although the Money et al. (1998) paper aggregated (for the sake of parsimony) the indicators into one measure of tie strength, the current study explicates the detail in the results by analyzing and presenting each measure of tie strength individually. Centrality has two measures, graph degree and graph between-ness, which were calculated for the entire network of the buying firm in the context of the 10 services examined in the Money et al. (1998) article. The data presented herein consider the centrality of the referral nodes that did the referring for *travel* services. The calculations of the indicators were done using UCINET IV (Borgatti et al. 1992), a software package that analyzes social networks. The results of these calculations and other measures were compared using one-way ANOVA for the 4 cells of the design. In addition, linear regression was used to examine the influence of company age and size on the results.

RESULTS

Since four of the 48 companies interviewed indicated they did not use a travel agent, the sample size available for analysis was 44. The fact that about 90% of the responses said they did use a travel agent indicates that the respondents, as a group, were heavy users of business travel services, especially through a travel agent. The ANOVA results in Table 1 indicate that national culture indeed has an effect on number of sources consulted ($F = 4.82$, $p = .034$), but that location of operation does not ($F = .15$, $p = .706$), supporting H1, but not H2. Regression results confirmed this analysis and show that the control variables of age and size, indicated by number of years in business, number of employees, and annual revenues, showed no significant effects on the number of sources consulted for travel agents.

Since the seven indicators of tie strength and two indicators of centrality could not be combined for purposes of the current research, results of ANOVA analyses on each individual indicator are shown in Table 2. For tie strength, the only indicator that was influenced by national culture was business importance ($F = 4.37$, $p = .066$). Perceived expertise was marginally influenced by culture ($F = 2.46$, $p = .152$), but none of the indicators was influenced by location of operation. Also, centrality indicators were not influenced by the independent variables. For space considerations, the cell means and regression results are not reported here, but none of the control variables was significant in predicting the influence of culture or location of any of the tie strength or centrality indicators.

DISCUSSION

Consistent with theory and the hypotheses forwarded herein, national culture was shown to influence the social network WOM referral activity of commercial buyers of travel services in the U.S. and Japan. That is, companies of collectivist, high context Japanese culture consulted more referral

TABLE 1. RESULTS
Number of Sources Consulted
n = 44

Independent Variables	*ANOVA Test Statistics*
National Culture:	F = 4.82 *
Location of Operation:	F = .15
R-squared = .11	

Regression Results	*Beta Coefficients*
National Culture	2.03 *
Location	0.68
Age of Company	0.01
Number of Employees	0.55
Annual Revenues	−1.04
R-squared = .13	

* $p < .05$

CELL MEANS (Std. Dev.):

NATIONAL CULTURE

		Japanese	American
LOCATION	Foreign	1. Japanese companies in U.S. $\overline{X}$ = .67 (.89)	2. American companies in Japan $\overline{X}$ = .08 (.29)
	Domestic	3. Japanese companies in Japan $\overline{X}$ = .34 (.64)	4. American companies in U.S. $\overline{X}$ = .20 (.42)

sources than American companies. The cell means in Table 1 also indicate this. The results would indicate that Japanese companies, whether operating in the U.S. and Japan, make more extensive use of referral networks than American companies. Most of the tie strength indicators were unaffected by culture, but one, business importance of the tie, was significant. Japanese, whose business culture values business relationships greatly, perhaps place

TABLE 2. RESULTS
Tie Strength and Centrality
n = 44

		Test Statistics	
Indicator		*National Culture*	*Location*
Tie Strength			
Duration	F =	.60	.64
R-squared = .10			
Frequency	F=	1.36	.04
R-squared = .16			
Social Importance	F=	.11	.24
R-squared = .03			
Business Importance	F =	4.37**	.01
R-squared = .36			
Likability	F =	.01	.96
R-squared = .10			
Trust	F=	.21	.09
R-squared = .03			
Expertise	F =	2.46	.96
R-squared = .25			
Centrality			
Degree	F=	.39	1.53
R-squared = .16			
Betweenness	F=	.11	.23
R-squared = .03			

** $p < .10$

the strength or context of ties above other criteria of relationship quality with their vendors. Apparently the placement of the referral sources in the WOM network is unaffected by culture, since the centrality results were not significant.

However, clearly the data held some surprises. Contrary to what theory would predict, location of operation had no effect on the referral process. That is, companies of both cultures, whether operating in their home country or abroad, showed no difference in the number of sources consulted nor the tie strength between buyer and referral source. Centrality was also unaffected by foreign vs. domestic location. The beta coefficient for location of operation was also not significant in the regression results.

What might account for the lack of location significance in the results?

First, the purchase of travel services, in an increasingly competitive global market, may at least seem to some corporate buyers to be more of a commodity purchase than it once was. That is, travel agents may be increasingly viewed as merely conduits to the airlines, hotels, and other services that are increasingly efficient and competitive in their approach to marketing, so the selection of a travel agent to source those services may be more of a convenience rather than a crucial decision. For example, in selecting an attorney or CPA, the client knows that a great deal of private information will be divulged and may give the referral process more consideration than when selecting a travel agent. Second and relatedly, specific to Japan, the affiliations between travel service providers could be breaking down somewhat (Sullivan 1995), increasingly giving the market the appearance of the deregulated airline industry or the long-distance phone service market (at least initially)–more competitively priced choices, resulting in less emphasis on the channel (travel agents) than on the end service providers themselves.

Limitations and Future Research

The results of the study are subject to the usual limitations of data collection with in-depth interviews (Aaker, Kumar, and Day 1998). Various respondents may interpret similar questions differently, give incomplete or cursory answers under the pressure of time, or may not choose to divulge what they consider to be sensitive information. In these particular interviews, since the nationality of the researcher (U.S.) was different from the nationalities of many of the respondents (Japanese), some subject bias towards a non-native researcher may have affected the results. Memory decay may also be present, since the companies were not startup operations when interviewed, in most cases. The average age of the participating companies was 5.8 years. The subjects were asked, on a 1 to 5 Likert scale (1 = poor recall, 5 = perfect recall) how well they recollected the events they described. The average response was 4.49. In spite of the self-report nature of the data, memory was likely to be enhanced by the fact that choosing the services to start a company happens only once and is likely more clearly remembered than normal day-to-day operating decisions. Future studies of this kind might address these limitations by interviewing multiple respondents about the same sourcing decisions. Collaborators native to the countries studied should also be used.

Hofstede's dimensions of national culture, while widely cited and applied, have not been exhaustively validated, and the similarity of his subjects (IBM employees) to those interviewed in the current study may be questioned. The small sample size (which might account for the small r-squared statistics) and number of countries may also limit the study's validity. While Japan and the U.S. represent a useful and interesting contrast, generalization to other countries in the international travel marketplace is difficult at best, or at least limited to countries of similar and analogous cultural and geographic distance. More companies included in future studies would increase the statistical power of the results. Since the study was conducted in only two regions of the two countries, generalizing to the U.S. and Japan should be done with caution. Therefore, the issue of subcultures should also be explored, since America is comprised of many (Kahle 1986), as is Japan. Examining the dependent variables as independent variables might also be interesting. Do, for example, companies that use more referrals remain more loyal to their travel agents than those who consult only the Yellow Pages?

Implications and Conclusion

These results of this study are important to travel marketers and academics because they provide some of the first side-by-side comparisons of how business-to-business travel purchases are made in the two large, important, but different markets of the U.S. and Japan. The broader implications of the article shed light on how marketers of travel services to businesses in two cultures and locations of great distance from each other might be more effective and how academics can continue researching the process. The addition of social networks theory and methods in the WOM setting to the study of travel purchase decisions is another theoretical contribution.

For tourism academics and practitioners of travel services alike, culture matters. Approaching a new market or research issue without considering the cross-cultural implications of the global nature of the travel industry could lead to misleading results or an unsuccessful marketing campaign. The influence of culture on the referral process cannot be overlooked, either as a barrier or opportunity, if understood correctly. A great deal of anecdotal evidence suggests differences in the Japanese business system, but the current research has explicated those differences specifically in the corporate travel industry. Traditional American marketing techniques to potential clients such as cold calling or mass mailings probably will meet with little success in Japan or cultures that are high in collectivism, uncertainty avoidance, and context.

However, the news for U.S. travel marketers is not all bad. The lack of significance in the tie strength and centrality results, for example, may indicate opportunities previously unconsidered. The fact that tie strength is unaffected by location and not influenced by culture for the most part means that American marketers may have a chance to break into referral networks for Japanese buyers in the U.S. and Japan. Despite its reputation as a closed market, apparently travel service marketers have the opportunity to do business in Japan through such networks. Even regarding Japanese buyers in the U.S., where Japanese typically bring their networking culture with them, apparently business travel vendors have a better chance at attracting clients than they might have previously thought possible.

Business-to-business travel marketers should proceed in carefully building relationships with buyers, as previous literature has suggested (Crotts and Wilson 1995), as with any international or cross-cultural business endeavor. The demise of the keiretsu system is greatly exaggerated by American news media; Japanese companies who have been doing business with each other for decades tend to stay with established ties. However, for those who intend to crack the Japanese corporate travel market both in Japan and with Japanese subsidiaries in the U.S., the results of the study should provide some direction and insight.

REFERENCES

Aaker, David A., V. Kumar, and George S. Day (1998), *Marketing Research*, sixth edition, New York: John Wiley & Sons.

Aaker, Jennifer L. and Durairaj Maheswaran (1997), "The Effect of Cultural Orientation on Persuasion," *Journal of Consumer Research*, 24 (December), 315-28.

Anderson, John R. (1983), *The Architecture of Cognition*. Cambridge, MA: Harvard University Press.

Anterasian, Cathy, John L. Graham, and R. Bruce Money (1996), "Are U.S. Managers Superstitious About Market Share?" *Sloan Management Review*, 37 (Summer), 67-77.

Batzer, Erich and Helmut Laumer (1989), *Marketing Strategies and Distribution Channels for Foreign Companies in Japan*. Boulder, CO: Westview Press.

Bavelas, Alex (1950), "Communications Patterns in Task-Oriented Groups," *Journal of the Acoustical Society of America*, 22, 725-30.

Beals, Ralph L. (1953), "Acculturation," in Alfred L. Kroeber, ed. *Anthropology Today*, University of Chicago Press.

Bearden, William O., Richard G. Netemeyer, and Jesse E. Teel (1989), "Measurement of Consumer Susceptibility to Interpersonal Influence," *Journal of Consumer Research*, 15 (March), 473-81.

Berry, Leonard L. and A. Parasuramen (1991), *Marketing Services: Competing Through Quality*. New York: The Free Press/Macmillan.

Borgatti, Stephen P., Steven Everett, and Linton C. Freeman. (1992), *UCINET IV*, version 1.0. Columbia, SC: Analytic Technologies.

Brown, Jacqueline Johnson and Peter H. Reingen (1987), "Social Ties and Word of Mouth Referral Behavior," *Journal of Consumer Research*, 14 (December), 350-62.

Carroll, Glenn R. and Albert C. Teo (1996), "On the Social Networks of Managers," *Academy of Management Journal*, 39 (April), 421-40.

Cateora, Philip R. and John L. Graham (1998), *International Marketing*, tenth edition, New York: Irwin McGraw-Hill.

Clark, Terry (1990), "International Marketing and National Character: A Review and Proposal for an Integrative Theory," *Journal of Marketing*, 54 (October), 66-79.

Cook, Thomas D. and Donald T. Campbell (1979), *Quasi-experimentation: Design and Analysis Issues for Field Settings*. Chicago: Rand McNally College Publishing.

Crocker, Kenneth E. (1986), "The Influence of the Amount and Type of Information on Individuals' Perception of Legal Services," *Journal of the Academy of Marketing Science*, 14 (4), 18-27.

Crotts, John C. (1999), "Consumer Decision Making and Prepurchase Information Search," in *Consumer Behavior in Travel and Tourism*, Yoel Mansfield and Abe Pizam, eds. Binghamton, N. Y.: The Haworth Press, Inc.

Crotts, John C. and David T. Wilson (1995), "An Integrated Model of Buyer-seller Relationships in the International Travel Trade," *Progress in Tourism and Hospitality Research*, 1 (2), 125-39.

Czinkota, Michael R. and Jon Woronoff (1986), *Japan's Market: The Distribution System*, New York: Praeger, 1986.

Dyer, Jeffrey H. and William G. Ouchi (1993), "Japanese-Style Partnerships: Giving Companies a Competitive Edge," *Sloan Management Review*, 34 (Fall), 51-63.

Feick, Lawrence F. and Linda L. Price (1987), "The Market Maven: A Diffuser of Marketplace Information," *Journal of Marketing*, 51 (January), 83-97.

File, Karen M., Ben B. Judd, and Russ A. Prince (1992), "Interactive Marketing: The Influence of Participation on Positive Word-of-Mouth Referrals," *Journal of Services Marketing*, 6 (Fall), 5-14.

File, Karen M., Dianne S.P. Cermack, and Russ A. Prince (1994a), "Word-of-mouth Effects in Professional Services Buyer Behavior," *Service Industries Journal*, 14 (July), 301-14.

File, Karen M., Judith L. Mack, and Russ A. Prince (1994b), "Marketing to a Family Firm: A New Consideration for Business-to-business Marketers," *Journal of Business and Industrial Marketing*, 9 (3), 64-72.

Frazier, Gary L., James D. Gill, and Sudhir H. Kale (1989), "Dealer Dependence Levels and Reciprocal Actions in a Channel of Distribution in a Developing County," *Journal of Marketing*, 53 (January), 50-69.

Freeman, Linton C., Douglas Roeder and Robert R. Mulholland (1980), "Centrality in Social Networks: II. Experimental Results," *Social Networks* 2, 119-41.

Frenzen, Jonathan K. and Harry L. Davis (1990), "Purchasing Behavior in Embedded Markets," *Journal of Consumer Research*, 17 (June), 1-15.

Frenzen, Jonathan K. and Kent Nakamoto (1993), "Structure, Cooperation, and the Flow of Market Information," *Journal of Consumer Research*, 20 (December), 360-75.

Gelb, Betsy and Madeline Johnson (1995), "Word-of-mouth Communication: Causes and Consequences," *Journal of Health Care Marketing*, 15 (Fall), 54-8.

Graham, John L. and Yoshihiro Sano (1989), *Smart Bargaining: Doing Business with the Japanese*, revised edition, New York: Harper & Row.

Granovetter, Mark (1973), "The Strength of Weak Ties," *American Journal of Sociology*, 78 (May), 1360-80.

Gronhaug, Kjell and John L. Graham (1987), "International Marketing Research Revisited," *Advances in International Marketing*, 2, 121-37.

Hall, Edward T. and Mildred Reed Hall (1987), *Hidden Differences*. Garden City, NY: Anchor/Doubleday.

Haywood, Michael K. (1989), "Managing Word-of-mouth Communications," *Journal of Services Marketing*, 3 (Spring), 55-67.

Hofstede, Geert (1980), *Culture's Consequences*. Beverly Hills: Sage Publications.

Hofstede, Geert (1991), *Cultures and Organizations–Software of the Mind*. London: McGraw-Hill.

Horsky, Dan and Karl Mate (1988). "Dynamic Advertising Strategies of Competing Durable Good Producers," *Marketing Science*, Vol.7 (fall), 356-67.

Horsky, Dan (1990), "A Diffusion Model Incorporating Product Benefits, Price, Income, and Information," *Marketing Science*, 9 (Fall), 342-65.

Ibarra, Herminia and Steven B. Andrews (1993), "Power, Social Influence and Sense Making: Effects of Network Centrality and Proximity on Employee Perceptions," *Administrative Science Quarterly*, 38 (June), 277-303.

Japan Travel Bureau (1994), *All About Japanese Overseas Travelers*. Tokyo: Japan Travel Bureau.

Johansson, Johny K. and Masaaki Hirano (1996), "Japanese Marketing in the Post-Bubble Era," International Executive, 38 (January/February), 33-51.

Kahle, Lynn R. (1986), "The Nine Nations of North America and the Value Basis of Geographic Segmentation," *Journal of Marketing*, 50 (April), 37-47.

Kale, Sudhir (1986), "Dealer Perceptions of Manufacturer's Power and Influence Strategies in a Developing Country," *Journal of Marketing Research*, 23 (November), 387-393.

Katz, Elihiu and Paul F. Lazarsfeld (1955), *Personal Influence*. Glencoe, IL: Free Press.

Kotler, Philip, John Bowen, and James Makens (1998), *Marketing for Hospitality and Tourism*. Upper Saddle River, NJ: Prentice Hall.

Mahajan, Vijay, Eitan Muller and Frank M. Bass (1990), "New Product Diffusion Models in Marketing: A Review and Direction for Research," *Journal of Marketing* 54 (January), 1-26.

March, James G. and Herbert A. Simon (1958), *Organizations*. New York: John Wiley & Sons, Inc.

March, Roger (1997). An Exploratory Study of Buyer-seller Relationships in International Tourism: The Case of the Japanese Wholesaler and Australian Suppliers. *Journal of Travel & Tourism Marketing*, 6 (1), 55-68.

McCracken, Grant D. (1988). *The long interview*. Newbury Park, CA: Sage Publications.

McGuire, William J. (1985), "Attitudes and Attitude Change," in *The Handbook of Social Psychology*, third edition, Gardner Lindzey and Elliot Aronson, eds. New York: Random House.

Money, R. Bruce and John C. Crotts (2000), "Buyer Behavior in the Japanese Travel Trade: Advancements in Theoretical Frameworks," *Journal of Travel & Tourism Marketing*, 9 (3), forthcoming.

Money, R. Bruce, Mary C. Gilly, and John L. Graham (1998), "Explorations of National Culture and Word-of-Mouth Referral Behavior in the Purchase of Industrial Services in the U.S. and Japan," *Journal of Marketing,* 62 (October), forthcoming.

Nairu, Tatsuhiko and David Flath (1993), "The Complexity of Wholesale Distribution Channels in Japan," in *The Japanese Distribution System, Opportunities and Obstacles, Structures and Practices,* Michael R. Czinkota and Masaaki Kotabe, eds. Chicago: Probus, 83-98.

Nakata, Cheryl and K. Sivakumar (1996), "National Culture and New Product Development: An Integrative Review," *Journal of Marketing,* 60 (January), 61-72

Ouchi, William (1981), *Theory Z: How American Business Can Meet the Japanese Challenge.* Boston: Addison-Wesley.

Pascale, Richard (1978), "Communication and Decision Making Across Cultures: Japanese and American Comparisons," *Administrative Science Quarterly,* 23 (March), 91-110.

Pascale, Richard and Anthony G. Athos (1981), *The Art of Japanese Management.* New York: Simon and Schuster.

Penaloza, Lisa (1994), "Atravensando Fronteras/Border Crossings: A Critical Ethnographic Exploration of the Consumer Acculturation of Mexican Immigrants," *Journal of Consumer Research,* 21 (June), 32-45.

Reingen, Peter H. and Jerome B. Kernan (1986), "Networks in Marketing: Methods and Illustration," *Journal of Marketing Research,* 13 (November), 370-8.

Reingen, Peter H., Brian L. Foster, Jacqueline Johnson Brown, and Stephen B. Seidman (1984), "Brand Congruence in Interpersonal Relations: A Social Network Analysis," *Journal of Consumer Research,* 11 (December), 771-83.

Ronchetto, John R. Jr., Michael D. Hutt, and Peter H. Reingen (1989), "Embedded Influence Patterns in Organizational Buying Systems," *Journal of Marketing,* 53 (October), 51-62.

Roth, Martin S. (1995), "The Effects of Culture and Socioeconomics on the Performance of Global Brand Image Strategies," *Journal of Marketing Research,* 32 (May), 163-75.

Ruan, Danching, Linton C. Freeman, Xinyuan Dai, Yunkang Pan, and Wenhong Zhang (1997), "On the Changing Structure of Social Networks in Urban China," *Social Networks,* 19, 75-89.

Sakaiya, Taichi (1993), *What is Japan? Transformations and Contradictions.* New York: Kodansha International.

Stayman, Douglas M. and Rohit Deshpande (1989), "Situational Ethnicity and Consumer Behavior," *Journal of Consumer Research,* 16 (December), 361-71.

Sullivan, J. (1995), "The Major Players in Asia's Travel Industry," *Travel and Tourism Analysis,* No. 1, 54-83.

Sullivan, Jeremiah and Richard B. Peterson (1988), "Factors Associated with Trust in Japanese-American Joint Ventures," *International Management Review,* 22 (2), 30-40.

Sultan, Fareena, John U. Farley, and Donald R. Lehmann (1990), "A Meta-analysis of Applications of Diffusion Models. *Journal of Marketing Research,* 27 (February), 70-7.

Takada, Hirokazu, and Dipak Jain (1991), "Cross-National Analysis of Diffusion of

Consumer Durable Goods in Pacific Rim Countries," *Journal of Marketing*, 55 (April), 48-54.

Tourism Industries (1998), "Surveys of Overseas Arrivals to the United States." Washington, DC: United States Department of Commerce.

Tse, David K., June Francis, and Jan Walls (1994), "Cultural Differences in Conducting Intra- and Inter-Cultural Negotiations: A Sino-Canadian Comparison," *Journal of International Business Studies*, 25 (3), 537-56.

Tse, David K., Kam-hon Lee, Ilan Vertinsky, and Donald A. Wehrung (1988), "Does Culture Matter? A Cross-Cultural Study of Executives' Choice, Decisiveness, and Risk Adjustment in International Marketing," *Journal of Marketing*, 52 (October), 81-95.

Ward, James C. and Peter H. Reingen (1990), "Sociocognitive Analysis of Group Decision Making among Consumers," *Journal of Consumer Research*, 17 (December), 245-62.

Webster, Cynthia (1988), "The Importance Consumers Place on Professional Services," *Journal of Services Marketing*, 2 (Winter), 59-70.

White, Douglas R. and Stephen P. Borgatti. (1994), "Centrality Measures for Oriented Graphs," *Social Networks*, 16, 335-46.

Williamson, Oliver E. (1975), *Markets and Hierarchies*. New York: The Free Press.

Yale, Laura J. (1989), "Individual Differences in Interpersonal Source Selection," doctoral dissertation, Graduate School of Management, University of California, Irvine.

Team Needs and Management of Multi-Ethnic Workgroups in Hotels

Helmut Waser
Nick Johns

SUMMARY. This study of multi-ethnic workgroups in two deluxe London hotels used an open-ended interview approach to obtain rich data from managers and their subordinates. Data was analysed using cultural dimensions identified by Hofstede and Trompenaars. Managers, who were from both individualistic and collectivistic national cultures expressed themselves in predominantly individualistic terms. In contrast, workers, regardless of their cultural background, spoke of their working relationships in a generally collectivistic way. They also said that they preferred to be managed in a collectivistic style, according to Trompenaars' categories. There was evidence that this clash of preferences caused conflict between workers and managers. Both managers and subordinates appeared to believe that a multi-ethnic workforce delivered a better quality service to a multi-ethnic clientèle than would a homogeneous staff team, but for different reasons. Managers mentioned the potential adaptability and innovativeness of a mix of different cultures. Workers spoke of multi-ethnic teams as being openminded, patient, understanding, sharing common goals and being a family. However, the collectivistic qualities of workgroups seemed to inspire workers from individualistic national cultures rather than the collectivistic nationalities. "Family" aspects of group work seemed inadequate for the latter, who tended to identify external factors as

Helmut Waser is affiliated with Norwich Hotel School, City College Norwich, Ipswich Road, Norwich NR2 2LJ, UK.

Nick Johns is Visiting Senior Research Fellow, Research Centre of Bornholm, Stenbrudsvej 55, 3730 Nexø, Denmark.

[Haworth co-indexing entry note]: "Team Needs and Management of Multi-Ethnic Workgroups in Hotels." Waser, Helmut, and Nick Johns. Co-published simultaneously in *International Journal of Hospitality & Tourism Administration* (The Haworth Press, Inc.) Vol. 1, No. 1, 2000, pp. 49-69; and: *Global Alliances in Tourism and Hospitality Management* (ed: John C. Crotts, Dimitrios Buhalis, and Roger March) The Haworth Press, Inc., 2000, pp. 49-69. Single or multiple copies of this article are available for a fee from The Haworth Document Delivery Service [1-800-342-9678, 9:00 a.m. - 5:00 p.m. (EST). E-mail address: getinfo@haworthpressinc.com].

49

responsible for their motivation. *[Article copies available for a fee from The Haworth Document Delivery Service: 1-800-342-9678. E-mail address: getinfo@haworthpressinc.com <Website: http://www.haworthpressinc.com>]*

KEYWORDS. Multi-ethnic workforce, cultural factors, employee motivation, management, leadership, management communication

INTRODUCTION

This article examines the impact of different national cultures upon the attitudes and dynamics of workgroups in hotels. Although a considerable body of literature is available about the cultures of individuals and nations there seems to be none dealing with the interactions of different cultures within a mixed group of service workers. The subject is of considerable importance in the hotel industry, which traditionally relies upon a multi-ethnic workforce, and faces an on-going challenge of how to lead such groups in a way that maximises service quality.

Culture and Workplace Relationships

Trompenaars (1993) defines culture in humanistic terms as a shared system of meanings, which influences or dictates a group of individuals' common perceptions, actions and values. Hofstede (1991) appears to take a somewhat more mechanistic view, defining culture as a "programming" of the mind that distinguishes the members of one group from another. Triandis et al. (1988) acknowledge culture as a "fuzzy construct" which they suggest should be analysed through dimensions of cultural variation in order to understand the way it relates to social psychological phenomena. The dimensionalisation of culture is accepted by both humanistic and mechanistic approaches. Hofstede (1991) identifies the dimensions: *individualism-collectivism; masculinity-femininity; uncertainty-avoidance;* and *high-low power distance;* while Trompenaars (1993) adds another four: *universalist-particularist; achievement-ascription; neutral-emotional; specific-diffuse.*

Hofstede's (1991) cultural dimensions represent central tendencies and according to him should not be used to predict the behaviour of individuals on the basis of their ethnicity. Hofstede (1991) notes that he has not been able to demonstrate differences between the members of professions on the basis of individualism/collectivism, although he has been able to do so for power distance. However, other authors have examined the applicability of national/ethnic cultural tendencies to individuals, and Triandis et al. (1988) claim that the personality dimension allocentrism/idiocentrism reflects the cultural collectivism/individualism dimension at the level of individual psychology. Hence they claim that individuals from collectivistic cultures characteristically subordinate their personal goals to the diffuse goals of a stable ingroup, while individualistic cultures are characterised by their members' independence from ingroups and also their detachment from them. Schwartz and Bilsky (1990) link personal values of security, prosocial and restrictive conformity to the collective motivational domain, while self-direction, achievement and enjoyment are linked to the individual motivational domain. Hence it can be argued that Hofstede's cultural dimensions offer a valuable approach to the understanding of human characteristics at the individual level.

Cultural dimensions which have been used to define managerial and subordinate behaviours include individualistic-collectivistic and high-low power distance (see Pizam, 1993). Individualistic cultures are held to emphasise individual initiative and achievement; leadership is the ideal, and work group members tend to value individual decisions. Within collectivistic cultures, membership rather than leadership is the goal and work group members value group decisions. In high power distance cultures, effective managers are seen as task-oriented, superiors are inaccessible, managers as power holders are entitled to privileges and most subordinates are dependent on their superiors. In contrast, in low power distance cultures, effective managers are people-oriented, participative-style leaders, superiors are accessible, superiors and subordinates have equal rights, and all members of the organisation are interdependent.

Ethnicity and Organisational Type

Cox and Blake (1991) propose a typology of organisations into *monolithic, pluralist* and *multicultural*. In the essentially ethnically homogeneous Monolithic organisations, employees may show racial prejudice towards ethnically dissimilar co-workers. Pluralist organisations employ moderate numbers of ethnically diverse individuals, but these tend to occupy lower levels of the hierarchy. Policies and procedures often exist in such organisations to support the ethnically diverse workforce, but managers may or may not have absorbed the intrinsic values of these policies. Multicultural organisations are defined as those which integrate an ethnically diverse workforce at all levels of the hierarchy, so that all employees manifest the values inherent in this integration. Larkey (1996) regards this typology as epitomising stages within a continuum of organisational development. She also extends it, to include smaller units within organisations, such as workgroups, but notes that need not be a complete match between workgroups within a given organisation, or between these subgroups and the whole organisation itself.

A related issue is that of corporate globalisation, for which Pizam (1993) describes two cultural stances. Organisations adopting a *convergent* stance expect to expand internationally without taking account of differing contexts, such as local ethnic culture. Those taking a *divergent* stance on the other hand make specific allowance for national ethnic characteristics in their different regional locations. In the cases examined by Pizam (1993) convergence was apparent at the macro level of the international organisation (i.e., its structure, specialisation of task and division of labour) whilst divergence typically occurred at the micro level of managerial and operational practice. The parallel with the Cox/Larkey typology is clear, and suggests that a need for control tends to keep organisations monolithic while practical and social pressures push workgroups towards a pluralistic, or even multicultural outlook.

Cultural Diversity and Communication

For Cox and Blake (1991) the cultural diversity of work groups is a resource which organisations may harness in order to gain competitive advantage, specifically through creativity and flexible adaptation to change. Thus they propose a "value-in diversity hypothesis" for which consensus appears to be growing in the literature. However, ethnically diverse workgroups need viable integration mechanisms and Maznevski (1994) suggests that organisations should seek to include individuals with similar abilities, to encourage mutual respect. She notes that groups with high ethnic diversity and poor integration perform less well than more homogeneous ones, and that effective communication is an important part of integration.

Communication difficulties arise between individuals who have very different ways of viewing the world but may be exacerbated by misinterpretation of organisational practices, or interpersonal reactions. For Kikoski (1993) effective communication depends upon the interacting parties taking account of each other's individual characteristics and cultural backgrounds. Individuals may recognise and react to one another's cultural diversity through either *categorisation* or *specification* (Larkey, 1996). The former process stereotypes people into broad categories, whereas specification recognises individual characteristics, including culture-group identity. Frequent outcomes of categorisation are prejudice, discrimination and poor communication. Larkey (1996) believes that specification occurs to a greater extent in multicultural organisations than in pluralistic ones.

According to Hall and Hall (1990) communication processes themselves are culturally determined. In collectivistic cultures *high context* communication predominates, characterised as being indirect, ambiguous and understated. In individualistic cultures *low context* communication is the norm and is characterised as being direct, explicit, open and precise. Thus differences in communication styles may also hinder the transfer of information and, ultimately, the integration of different cultures.

Workgroups and Leadership

Cox et al. (1991) suggest that ethnically diverse groups face a task more co-operatively than "all-Anglo" groups, and that managers should find ways of engaging this diversity. However, ethnicity or gender may be irrelevant to workgroup function in cohesive workgroups, focused on common goals, even when cultural value differences persist. In such cases organisational and workgroup practices tend to dominate, creating a unified group culture and sense of equality (Larkey, 1996).

Adair (1983) describes the functional effectiveness of a leader in terms of three areas: *task needs, individual needs* and *team maintenance needs* within the work group. Other models of leadership acknowledge the situational dependency of team needs (Hersey and Blanchard, 1988; Nicholls, 1985), but they generally agree that effective leadership must meet the needs of subordinates as well as the demands of the task. According to Hofstede (1991) "leadership" exists in a complementary relationship to "subordinateship" and the dynamics between these qualities exhibit cultural variation. For example, leadership appears to be embedded in group structure to a greater degree in collectivistic cultures than in individualistic ones (Smith and Bond 1993) and, as one might expect, views of leadership and power often vary in terms of power distance and uncertainty avoidance dimensions. Managers need to respond to these cultural differences as well as to task and team needs in order to lead multi-ethnic workgroups effectively (Tait, 1996).

The complexity of balancing multi-ethnic, individual and team needs can be illustrated by examples from the literature. Ingram (1997) comments that teams develop a camaraderie that allows them to develop a sense of family and team spirit, typical values of collectivist cultures. He also reports that team-working in the hospitality industry fosters empowerment. However, Baum (1995) notes that *high context* cultures in Europe have high masculinity and uncertainty avoidance indexes which may be incompatible with staff empowerment. Roper and Hampton (1997) suggest that staff from high context societies may have a need to be told personally what to do, whilst low context managers prefer to give them clear written instructions.

Natale et al. (1994) maintain that ethnic culture influences individuals' level of commitment to work. In this respect, Hofstede (1991) proposes that Maslow's needs hierarchy is culturally variable. For example, belongingness will prevail over esteem in a feminine culture such as that in Denmark or Portugal and esteem over belongingness in a masculine culture such as Japan, Ireland or the USA. Therefore motivating the workforce by fulfilling individual or team needs could be a complex task with a multi-ethnic workgroup. Individuals within the team would *a priori* be expected to bring a cultural as well as a personal needs hierarchy into the workgroup. Those from collectivistic cultures for instance may be willing to forgo personal needs for goal achievement but this would seem less likely for workers from individualistic cultures.

Large hotels in many western cities typically employ an ethnically diverse workforce at middle to low levels of the organisation (Baum, 1996) and would thus be pluralist rather than multicultural according to Larkey's (1996) typology. Numerous authors have pointed out the importance of effective communication in the hospitality industry, where staff turnover is a common problem and collaboration and responsiveness are required for the effective delivery of customer service. There is clearly also a need to address the cultural aspects of communication and teamwork (Brownell, 1992).

In fact, little is known about the way a mixture of different ethnicities impacts upon the team culture of workgroups and it seems likely that this must have important consequences, for both the management and motivation of such teams. The research described here used a qualitative approach to examine cultural interactions between workers and managers in two London hotels, both of which employed staff from very diverse national backgrounds. Objectives of the study were to identify how managers and workers regarded each other, to see how workgroup cultures reflected the "component" cultures within them and to discover what lessons needed to be learned in order to make the management of such groups more effective.

DATA

This study was carried out at an 800 bedroom, four star hotel close to Heathrow Airport and a 300 bedroom five star hotel in central London, selected because of the ethnic heterogeneity of their workforces. Data consisted of transcripts of recorded open-ended interviews from a total of 42 workers (from 17 different nationalities) and 24 managers (from a total of 9 nationalities) at the two hotels.

Permission to interview staff was obtained from Head Office, and separately from senior management at each establishment. Interviewees were approached singly either at their workplace or in the canteen and were aware that their comments were being tape-recorded. Interviews lasted 15 to 60 minutes with an average time of about 30 minutes. The shorter interviews occurred either because work interrupted the discussion or because the individual was uneasy about the interview. Interviews were open ended, but followed a predetermined framework, with staff being first encouraged to talk about themselves, the culture that they came from and the work environment. Informants were encouraged to talk about working relationships with other workers, with managers/subordinates and with guests within a multiethnic environment.

The methodological principles of grounded theory (Strauss and Corbin 1990) were used to derive concepts and theory systematically from the empirical data in a series of stages. In the first stage, statements were categorised into those where workers spoke about their fellow workers and those where they discussed their managers. Next, core categories of meaning were identified within these initial groups and within these, the statements were sorted according to whether they expressed collectivistic or individualistic ideals, this being a subcategory that suggested itself from the raw data. It also seemed worthwhile to compare the statement categories with those identified in Trompenaars' (1993) study of workgroup cultures. At this point it seemed that there was a discrepancy between the cultures of the workgroups and the expected cultural characteristics of the individuals within them. Therefore the statements were further sub-grouped as "collectivistic" or "individualistic" on the basis of informants' nationalities, using Hofstede's (1991) IDV classification list for 50 countries and 3 regions (p. 53). Results of the whole analysis are shown in Table 1.

Since communication emerged clearly as a category in the analysis, it seemed likely that, besides the individualistic/collectivistic ethnicity factor, informants' English language ability might be an important variable. Figure 1 shows the ethnic collectivistic/individualistic breakdown (based on national origin) together with the proportion of native English-speakers within the sample. Twelve percent of statements by individuals from collectivistic national cultures about their fellow workers were categorised as individualistic in character, while 64% of statements by workers from individualistic nationalities were classified as collectivistic. The classifications were carried out

TABLE 1. Statement categories from the present study compared with "collectivistic" workgroup characteristics identified by Trompenaars (1993) and Hofstede's IDV nationality types.

Characteristics of "collectivistic" workgroups	Empirical categories in this study	Interviewees' Nationality type in each category
Integrate authority figure	Communication, Harmony/patience	C: 5, I: 1I: 1
Esprit de corps	Learning, Harmony/patience	C: 5, I: 1I: 2
Low job turnover	Learning	C: 1, I: 2
Whole group performance	Learning, Common goal, Harmony/patience	C: 2, I: 3C: 9I: 7
Superordinate goals	Common goal	C: 5
Whole workgroup	Family	I: 3

Key: I/C = "individualistic"/"collectivistic" workers grouped by Hofstede's (1991) IDV index. Number refers to statements which meet both Trompenaars' and present research criteria.

FIGURE 1. Characteristics of worker and manager population

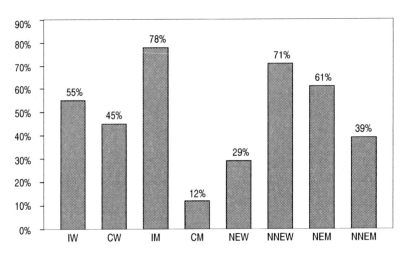

Key

"Individualist" workers	IW
"Collectivist" workers	CW
"Individualist" managers	IM
"Collectivist" managers	CM
Native English workers	NEW
Non-native English workers	NNEW
Native English managers	NEM
Non-native English managers	NNEM

independently by two individuals and compared in order to minimise subjective bias.

From the managers' comments emerged the subcategories *external influence, perception, communication* and *group interaction*. In order to achieve comparability with the workers' data, the statements were likewise subcategorised on their face-value individualism/collectivism and on the basis of the interviewee's ethnic culture.

FINDINGS

Workers' Views

The principal categories emerging from workers' statements about their co-workers were: *common goal, adjustment and learning, harmony/patience* and *family*. Workers' statements about their managers gave rise to the categories: *feelings*, *communication* and *positional attitude*. These category sets are discussed below.

Comments About Co-Workers

The *common goal* category contained 13 statements, exclusively from workers from "collectivistic" nationalities (according to the IDV). They demonstrated that some workers used the idea of an external goal to help them overcome negative aspects of their work, their working conditions and their colleagues. The word "we" occurred in most of the statements, which suggested that these "collectivistic" workers were using an external goal as a device for minimising internal group differences. It was the goal which focused the group, while the internal dynamics of the team were of secondary importance and the multi-ethnic nature of the team was ignored, for example:

> *The common goal tells you what you must do, if you don't do it you will lose your job.* (Nigerian room service waiter)

> *You cannot like one person or another but you have to work together, put bad feelings away.* (Turkish concierge)

The *adjustment and learning* category contained 14 statements, six from workers from "individualistic" nationalities and eight from "collectivistic" workers. Their statements showed that they viewed learning as a positive aspect of a multi-ethnic workgroup, compared to the more negative aspects of the *common goal* approach. The following statements exemplify this category:

> *You can always learn from different people . . . you work with many different nationalities they all have something interesting experienced [sic]. . . Everybody is different and it is fascinating.* (Cameroons valet)

> *It is difficult to tell your friends to do things in the right way and you must learn the right way to tell your friend so he understands and feels good.* (French waiter)

The *harmony/patience* category contained five statements, all from "individualistic" workers, who implied that they found their work group mutually very supportive. Language problems might have been expected to cause annoyance and frustrations but this did not seem to occur, perhaps because so many of the group members had language difficulties. In fact communication seemed to be enhanced where native English speakers had to slow their speech and listen more carefully. The struggle to use English as a common language was identified as a vehicle which brought different nationalities together and hence assisted team building, as in the following statement:

> *It is a matter of being patient. Being English I had to slow down, be patient and understanding.* (English commis)

> *Around here it is getting better because everyone slows down and starts to listen.* (Canadian chef)

The *family* category also contained five statements, all made by workers from "individualistic" nationalities. The absence of comments from "collectivistic" workers was surprising and perhaps meant that there were no recognisable "family" characteristics within their work groups. The "individualistic" respondents said that they perceived within their teams: respect, good communication, smiling, sticking together, and that this created a sense of *family*, for example:

> *It is like a big family. Everyone is really close.* (English commis)

> *We are all a big family.* (English waitress)

> *It gives people a sense of belonging somewhere yes you work here and you belong to the hotel.* (Danish room maid)

Comments About Managers

The *communication* category contained 17 statements, eight from "individualistic" workers and nine from "collectivistic" nationalities, all of which viewed effective communication as a key aspect of good management. Respondents' difficulties with spoken English may have contributed to these feelings, but overall the statements seemed to go beyond simple language problems. They included a desire to understand the working situation, and to participate in decision making, for example:

> *We can't read their minds . . . need to talk to us more . . . not wait and wait until we make more mistakes.* (Kenyan housekeeper)

Statements in this category also highlighted management's poor communication and unappreciativeness of respondents' work and suggested some loss of motivation. Staff said that managers addressed them in a formal way and only if there was a problem or issue to do with the job. They felt that this had a negative impact on them and indicated that managers saw them as less than human. They complained that there was little sociable to smooth the process of work, for example:

> *I feel like a number, and you are never thanked for what you do. Not asked for your opinions.* (Maltese receptionist)

The *positional attitude* category contained eight statements, six from "individualistic" workers and two from "collectivistic" nationalities, who felt that managers looked down upon them and did not appreciate their work. In some cases their managers did not even bother to learn their names. They commented that managers did not understand them, for example:

> *All managers have the same negative attitude to their employees. You have to see how they look at us . . . they look down on us.* (French concierge)

> *How can you be a manager of people if you don't know anything about human behaviour?* (Maltese receptionist)

The *feelings* category contained three statements from workers from "individualistic" nationalities, and expressed a desire for managers to consider the feelings of those that they managed. Statements typically talked about respect and closeness, and the motivating effect of these qualities, for example:

> *We feel he likes us and that motivates you.* (French supervisor)

Summary of Workers' Comments

Workers from both "collectivistic" and "individualistic" nationalities mentioned the value of learning in multi-ethnic situations, but "collectivistic" nationalities also sometimes attempted to deny responsibility for the social dynamics of the work group by focusing upon external goals of the work itself. "Individualistic" informants felt that work groups were supportive and that they themselves contributed to this by their patience and forbearing. They also perceived their workgroups to have "family" qualities, but these were not acknowledged by "collectivistic" workers.

Workers from both "individualistic" and "collectivistic" nationalities regarded communication as a key issue in management and wished to be more involved in the work and decision-making. They also desired more social and interpersonal contact with managers. Both groups felt their managers took inadequate interest in their work and gave staff inadequate recognition and acknowledgement. In addition "individualistic" workers felt that feelings were important, though not always considered by managers.

Thus the two cultural groups felt similarly about their managers, but very differently about their work groups. It was as if the "collectivistic" tendency of the work groups surpassed the expectations of "individualistic" workers, resulting in positive feelings of support. However it seemed to be inadequate for the needs of "collectivistic" workers, who tended to concentrate upon other issues, such as external goals, for motivation. Nevertheless a "collectivistic" tendency was clearly evident from all workers with respect to their requirements from management.

MANAGERS' VIEWS

The overwhelming majority of managers were from "individualistic" national cultures, and in contrast to the workers they made statements which were predominantly individualistic in character. They were also very much concerned with the task focus of the work. The categories which emerged from their statements about their subordinates were *external influence, perception, communication* and *group interaction*, discussed below.

The *external influence* category contained only two comments, both made by manager/supervisors with "collectivistic" backgrounds. An example was:

> *In a responsible position I need to get on with people. I am responsible for my department so I must accept everyone's culture.* (Algerian head chef)

This feeling of "having to adjust" was evidently not shared by other managers in the sample. The need to act was apparently being externalised from the individual onto the organisation, seemingly paralleling the *common goal* category identified among the workers' comments.

The *perception* category contained seven statements dealing with the way managers said they saw their workers. Five were from "individualistic" and two from "collectivistic" individuals, based on national cultures. "Individualistic" statements showed a tendency to deal with different nationalities "en masse" even where they seemed overtly concerned with individuals, for example:

> *I know I can rely on that person to do this not because he is Greek or Italian or French but because I know that I have seen him do it before and he can do it again.* (Canadian head concierge)

Some openly admitted to generalising national cultures in their minds and to using their knowledge of staff ethnicity to their own advantage, for example:

> *Asians, if there is a dirty job, it is easier to tell them rather than Europeans who may argue. I use my cultural knowledge to my advantage.* (Irish bar manager)

Collectivistic statements in this category expressed interpersonal feelings much more and tended to deal with workers as individuals:

I think they are people-people, they are people who like people, so they make a point of understanding and being helpful with other people. (Canadian head concierge)

It is interesting to consider this comment in the light of the previously quoted statement by this same individual. Despite the "collectivistic" stance of this statement, it is clearly still concerned with relationships between "others," i.e., as an outsider towards a group to which the speaker does not belong.

The *communication* category contained four statements, all individualistic in character. Some managers felt that they adapted their style to multi-ethnic workers' needs, but were perhaps unrealistically optimistic about their efforts:

I try to treat everybody equally and in a fair way. The only time cultural background comes into it is maybe when it has to do with language differences, where you have to make allowances and be more explanatory. (English human resource officer)

Others said they altered their communication style to match management norms, rather than to meet the needs of their workers:

You have to say please. In Holland you say "let's do it" and that is it. Sometimes I do it the Dutch way here and it looks like you are aggressive, you are hard, you look like a dictator. (Dutch management trainee)

The *group interaction* category contained a total of eleven comments: seven from "individualistic" and four from "collectivistic" managers. Collectivistic statements dealt with interpersonal feelings within the leadership role:

You are tired, you have to take the time for your staff, this is real leadership. You have to show them you care. (English food and beverage manager)

Alternatively they expressed positive views of ethnic diversity:

It is like putting a jigsaw puzzle together and you can see they are all working well together. (Egyptian restaurant manager)

At the same time such comments kept a distance between this manager and his workers. Individualistic statements could also express a positive view of ethnic diversity, but did so in a somewhat more manipulative way:

Their own culture adds little touches and little innovative ways that they have learned in their own culture we bring it together and make it better. It is like a melting pot and this is what I call progress. (Irish bar manager)

Some of the "individualistic" statements also expressed the hope that ethnic diversity in itself was not a problem, or that organisational systems and procedures were adequate to deal with it:

There might be people who don't like each other but I don't think they can't work with each other. (Irish trainee manager)

If the environment is well managed and if people feel that there are systems to protect them then they speak up if something goes wrong. (Irish trainee manager)

Summary of Managers' Comments

Managers showed a tendency to focus upon task and group needs rather than those of individuals. Probably this was because the former require lower-level managerial or administrative skills than the leadership skills or qualities that are needed to address individual and cultural needs. Managers also seemed unprepared for dealing with a multi-ethnic work force, either ignoring such issues in their responses or expressing unjustified hope that it was not a problem, or could be dealt with under existing practice.

Like the workers, managers agreed that ethnic and cultural diversity could be an advantage. At an individual level diversity was "interesting" and "stimulating," while for the organisation it could provide "new ideas" or "compliant workers." The research data suggested that there was a gap between the way the two groups thought about communication, and this seemed to be a key issue in the leadership of multi-ethnic groups.

DISCUSSION

In the hotels of the present study there was noticeably greater ethnic diversity among workers than among managers, and though in principle policies and procedures were in place to improve employment of minorities, observable prejudice manifested itself in subtle forms. Thus both hotels can be considered *pluralistic* in terms of Cox and Blake's organisational typology. A number of managers' statements recalled Larkey's (1996) comment about this type of organisation: "majority members often truly believe that they hold no prejudice; diversity is seen as a problem to be managed" (p. 466)

In contrast, the workgroups showed many truly multicultural characteristics. The diverse cultural membership was comparatively well-integrated and common values were in evidence. Participative practices were apparent and some individuals reported a "family" atmosphere. It may be of practical interest to study the development of such multiculturally-focused groups on a longitudinal basis, since they are likely to play a significant role in the transition of organisations from a pluralistic to a more truly multicultural work environment.

Statements by managers about their staff showed evidence of categorisation of individuals, an approach to ethnic diversity which predominates in monolithic and pluralistic organisations. In truly multicultural communities one would expect much greater evidence of specification, which in the present study occurred much more within workgroups than between managers and workers. A key stage in the transition from a pluralistic to multicultural work environment ought to be the widespread manifestation of specification in interpersonal perception. However this is unlikely to occur until managers (who currently seem to lag behind the workforce in this respect) embrace the need to change. Systems and procedures also play a part. Larkey (1996) notes that reward systems which focus upon the individual encourage categorisation and suggests that whole group reward systems are more appropriate in developing a culture of specification.

A striking observation of this study was that the workgroups seemed markedly more collectivistic in outlook than would have been predicted from the national ethnicities from which they were composed. This must of course be treated with caution since it relies on an arbitrary discontinuity between individualists and collectivists at the mid-point of Hofstede's IDV continuum. Individualistic and collectivistic tendencies undoubtedly vary between individuals of the same nationality, and ethnicity also varies between different regions. Finally, this was only one cultural dimension chosen from several possible ones. Its justification in the present study lies in its spontaneous emergence from the qualitative data, but this is not to say that other dimensions, or an analysis based upon several simultaneous dimensions might not provide a more powerful variable for discriminating between different cultural types. Despite this, the result is of interest, since it is grounded in empirical data. It is also consistent with Ingram's (1997) experience that workgroups develop values which can be classified as collectivist, and with Brownell's (1992) contention that team spirit must form in hotels under the pressure to deliver excellent service. It should be borne in mind that the present study set out to provide an illuminative view of multiethnic hotel workgroups, and a complementary quantitative study would be required to test this interesting hypothesis.

Hopkins (1997) suggests that organisations which suddenly experience an influx of different ethnicities suffer a kind of moral stress that he calls an "ethics paradigm shift." Hotels have a long history of employee diversity which at the time of writing is in fact changing comparatively slowly. They should thus experience the minimum of such stress, maintaining relatively stable organisational cultures and resisting transition towards a multicultural state. There was evidence of such stability among the statements collected in the present research. It seems unlikely that timely transition will in fact occur unless purposeful action is taken to facilitate the transition from a pluralist to a multicultural work environment.

Leadership styles are influenced by a number of factors, including educational experiences, and organisational, as well as cultural, characteristics. The evidence collected in this study suggests a need to address the specific needs of different cultural groupings, as well as the team, task and individual needs suggested by Adair. Thus improvements in overall performance might result from a better understanding of how "leadership style" and "group function" (Adair, 1983) interact in a multi-ethnic setting. Figure 2 shows how leadership, individual needs, and group needs may be connected. It seems likely that a shift in leadership styles might aid the transition from pluralist to multicultural organisational milieu.

Workers' concerns about communication in the present study recall the observations of Maznevski (1994) who also regards this as a key ingredient for the successful functioning of ethnically diverse workgroups. In the present study managers clearly did not communicate in ways appropriate to the needs of the workers. Morand (1995) notes that all cultures have sets of conventions that register politeness, which provide a buffer to ease interpersonal friction. However, these vary widely between cultures and mismatches in behaviour often cause severe problems of inter-cultural misunderstanding. Some elements of workers' discontent with managers' communication in the present study fell within the general domain of 'politeness.' Moreover, Larkey (1996) proposes that specification is more likely to occur where managers and workers mutually adjust to each others' communication style. This is conceived as shown in Figure 3, where the circle represents perceptions of the whole ethnically diverse work environment, while the square and triangle represent the perceptions of individualistic and collectivistic individuals respectively. The job of largely individualistic managers can be seen as moving their own perception outwards towards the limits of the circle. At the same time they should seek to reduce the constraining effect of their own perceptions upon their collectivistic workers and workgroups, so that the

FIGURE 2. Suggested impact of leadership style on collectivistic-type work-group performances

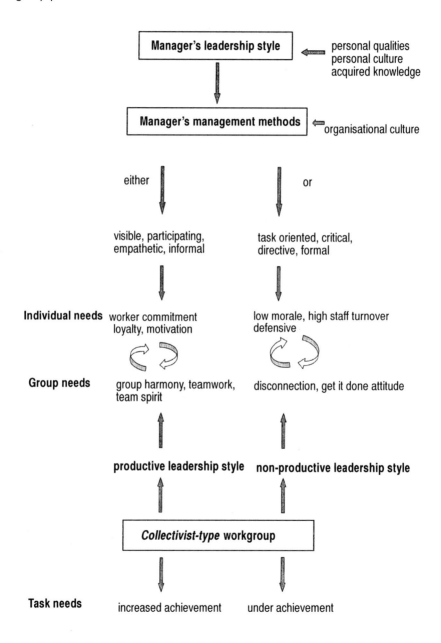

FIGURE 3. Diagrammatic representation of the overlap between the ideal perception of a workgroup by its members (circle) and the natural "individualistic" (square) and "collectivistic" (triangle) perceptions. Managers (a) should aim to expand their own perceptions to fit the ideal as far as possible (b) but also to allow their "collectivistic" workers freedom to develop their own fit.

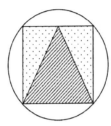
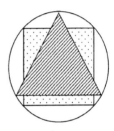

(a) "Individualistic" managers have a less than ideal perception of the workgroup and tend to restrict "collectivists" to this view.

(b) "Individualistic" managers develop their perception of the workgroup but are still restricting "collectivists."

(c) "Individualistic" managers have optimised their perception of the workgroup and also allow "collectivists" to do so.

latters' triangle can actually emerge beyond the square of individualistic views and contribute to the overall perception in its own right.

Of the various theories of intergroup relations, van Øudenhoven's (1989) *contact hypothesis* is probably the one most relevant to reducing ethnic friction in the workplace. This suggests that the key to reducing prejudice is the achievement of equal status contact between majority and minority groups in the pursuit of common goals. In this respect it was evident that managers in the present study contributed to prejudice by taking a dismissive or negative attitude to their workers, or even by manipulating them (as with the Asians who were more likely to be asked to do the dirty work). Subtle issues such as these illustrate how far industry has to go to achieve full cultural harmony at the multi-ethnic workplace.

RECOMMENDATIONS

Workplace Developments

The evidence presented here suggests that although the hotels in the study had well established multi-ethnic workforces, extensive cultural change would be necessary in order to achieve a smooth transition from a pluralistic to truly multicultural organisation. It is well known that such change has to occur on a "top down" basis, and that considerable resources are required to initiate and maintain it (see for example Johns and Chesterton, 1994 and Johns and Wildblood, 1994). One of the objectives of such a change may be the development of a culture in which managers can see the value of integrating themselves into the workgroup. In other words managers, who in the present study were "individualistic" in outlook, both by nationality and in the attitudes they exhibited, should be encouraged to develop a more "collectivistic" perspective. Manifestations of this would be:

- Managers speaking to their subordinates as though they were individuals rather than just operative, i.e., asking after their families, hobbies, social life, etc.
- Managers adapting their communication style to make it more informal and friendly, less abrupt and autocratic.
- Managers sharing aspects of the decision-making process and being more open about the logic behind work patterns.
- Managers demonstrating themselves the operational knowledge and skills that they require from their subordinates.
- The whole organisation emphasising teamwork and team needs, for example by changing from an "employee of the month" reward system common in many hotels, to a "team of the month."

Research Notes and Suggestions for Further Work

The qualitative approach described here was necessitated by the objectives of the study and by the conditions under which access to the research site was granted. Open-ended responses were obtained with the minimum of prompting by the researcher and the questions and prompts used were of a general nature, in order to draw out a spontaneous picture from the respondents. Analysis was inductive in nature, grounded upon the statements of the respondents, an approach which is generally accepted to minimise observer bias in this type of work (e.g., Glaser and Strauss, 1967).

Validity in such a study is obtained through the depth and complexity of the data, rather than its quantity. However, the relatively small samples necessitated by in-depth qualitative interviewing cannot claim to provide more than a glimpse into the situation. A quantitative study, based upon larger samples, and investigating a greater variety of workgroups and industrial sectors would be necessary to test the hypotheses generated by the present work.

Multicultural aspects of leadership and organisational development might be examined and simultaneously enhanced through the use of action research (see also suggestions by Teare, 1997 and Larkey, 1996). This technique might make managers more aware of their communication practices and of the expectations of *multi-ethnic* workgroups.

This study has largely ignored the issue of intercultural exchanges between service staff and customers, yet these are potentially a very important ingredient of service delivery and hence of service quality, offering a good deal of scope for further work. Ultimately it may be that findings of the type discussed in the present paper will also shed light upon inter-ethnic service encounters, adding a further dimension to existing knowledge of service perceptions.

REFERENCES

Adair, J. (1983) *Effective Leadership*, Pan Books.

Baum,T. (1995) *Managing Human Resources in the European Tourism and Hospitality Industry: A Strategic Approach*, Chapman Hall, London.

Baum, T. (1996) "Managing cultural diversity in tourism," *Tourism Intelligence Papers*, British Tourist Authority/English Tourist Board, pp. 77-84.

Brownell, J. (1992) "Hospitality Managers' Communication Practices," *International Journal of Hospitality Management*, Vol. 11, No. 2, pp. 111-128.

Cox, T.H. and Blake, S. (1991) "Managing Cultural Diversity: Implications for Organisational Competitiveness," *Academy of Management Executive*, Vol. 5, No. 3, pp. 45-56.

Cox, T.H., Lobel, S.A. and McLeod, P.L (1991) "Effects of ethnic group cultural differences on co-operative and competitive behaviour on a group task," *Academy of Management Journal*, Vol. 34, No. 4, pp. 827-847.

Glaser, B. and Strauss, A.L. (1967) *The Discovery of Grounded Theory: Strategies for Qualitative Research*, Aldine, New York.

Hall, E.T. and Hall, M.R. (1990) *Understanding Cultural Differences*, Intercultural Press, Maine, USA.

Hersey, P. and K. Blanchard (1988). *Management of Organizational Behavior, 5th Ed.,* Prentice Hall.

Hofstede, G. (1991) *Cultures and Organisations: Software of the Mind*, Harper Collins Publishing, London.

Hopkins, W.E. (1997). *Ethical Dimensions of Diversity.* London: Sage Publications.

Ingram, H. (1997) "Performance Management: Processes, Quality and Teamworking," *International Journal of Contemporary Hospitality Management*, Vol. 9, No. 7, pp. 295-303.

Ivey, A. E., Ivey, M.B. and Simek-Downing, L. (1987) *Counselling and Psychotherapy: Integrating Skills, Theory, and Practice. 2nd Ed.* Englewood Cliffs, NJ: Prentice Hall.

Johns, N. and Chesterton, J. (1994) "ICL Kidsgrove: snapshot of a changing culture," in *Achieving Quality Performance: Lessons from British Industry*, Ed. R. Teare, Cassell, 1994, pp. 79-110.

Johns, N. and Wildblood, S. (1994) "Beyond the yellow brick road: the continuing search for quality at D2D," *Managing Service Quality*, Vol. 4, No. 3, pp. 30-35.

Kikoski, J.E. (1993). "Effective Communication in the Workplace: Models for Public Sector Managers & Theorists." *Personnel Administration Quarterly*, Vol. 7, No. 7, pp. 84-95.

Larkey, L.K. (1996) "Toward a theory of communicative interactions in culturally diverse workgroups," *Academy of Management Review*, Vol. 21, No. 2, pp. 463-491.

Maznevski, M. (1994) "Understanding our differences: performance in decision-making groups with diverse members," *Human Relations*, Vol. 47, No. 5, pp. 531-552.

Morand, D.A. (1995) "Politeness as a universal variable in cross-cultural managerial Communication," *The International Journal of Organisational Analysis*, Vol. 3, No. 4, pp. 52-74.

Natale, S.M., Sora, S.A., and Madden, T. (1994) "Corporations without national boundaries," *Cross-Cultural Management: An International Journal*, Vol. 2, pp. 3-12.

Nicholls, J.R. (1985) "A new approach to situational leadership," *Leadership and Organisational Development Journal*, Vol. 6, No. 4, pp. 2-7.

Pizam, A. (1993) "Managing cross-cultural hospitality enterprises," in *The International Hospitality Industry: Organisational and Operational Issues*, Eds. Jones, P. and Pizam, A., Pitman, London.

Roper, A. and Hampton, A. (1997) "The multi-cultural management of international hotel groups," *International Journal of Hospitality Management*, Vol. 16, No. 2, pp. 147-159.

Schwartz, S.H. and Bilsky, W. (1990) Toward a Theory of the Universal content and Structure of Values: Extensions and Cross-Cultural Replications. *Journal of Personality and Social Psychology*. Vol. 58, No. 5, pp. 878-891.

Smith, P.B. and Bond, M.H. (1993) *Social Psychology Across Cultures: Analysis and Perspectives*, Harvester Wheatsheaf, Herts, UK.

Strauss, A. and Corbin, J. (1990) *Basics of Qualitative Research. Grounded Theory Procedures and Techniques*, Sage, London.

Tait, R. (1996) "The attributes of leadership," *Leadership & Organisation Development Journal*, Vol. 17, No. 1, pp. 27-31.

Teare, R. (1997) "Supporting managerial learning in the workplace," *International Journal of Contemporary Hospitality Management*, Vol. 9, No. 7, pp. 304-314.

Triandis, H., Bontempo, R., and Villareal, M.J. (1988) "Individualism and collectivism: cross-cultural perspectives on self-ingroup relationships," *Journal of Personality and Social Psychology*, Vol. 54, No. 2, pp. 323-338.

Trompenaars, F. (1993) *Riding the Waves of Culture: Understanding Cultural Diversity in Business*. Nicholas Brealey Publishing, London.

Van Øudenhoven, J.P. and T.M. Willemsen (1989). *Ethnic Minorities*. Amsterdam: Swebs Zeitlinger.

Tastes of Niagara:
Building Strategic Alliances
Between Tourism and Agriculture

David J. Telfer

SUMMARY. Given the diverse structure within the tourism industry, the establishment and maintenance of strategic alliances has become an important approach to remaining competitive and innovative. The relationship between tourism and agriculture is complex and the purpose of this paper is to investigate "Tastes of Niagara: A Quality Food Alliance," an evolving strategic alliance among the Region's food producers, processors, distributors, hotels, wineries, restaurants and chefs. The objective of the alliance is to promote the use of local products in the tourism industry. Key informant interviews were conducted with members of the alliance documenting the importance and difficulties in establishing and maintaining successful strategic alliances. *[Article copies available for a fee from The Haworth Document Delivery Service: 1-800-342-9678. E-mail address: getinfo@haworthpressinc.com <Website: http://www.haworthpressinc.com>]*

KEYWORDS. Agritourism, strategic alliances, Niagara Region

INTRODUCTION

The complexity of the tourism industry makes the establishment and maintenance of successful relationships critical. From local to international

David J. Telfer is affiliated with the Department of Recreation and Leisure Studies, Brock University, St. Catharines, Ontario, Canada.

This research was undertaken with a SSHRC research grant and with the assistance of Silvana R. Auld and Christa Pinkpank. Special thanks to Bob Kuhns and Johanna McDougal of Tastes of Niagara.

[Haworth co-indexing entry note]: "Tastes of Niagara: Building Strategic Alliances Between Tourism and Agriculture." Telfer, David J. Co-published simultaneously in *International Journal of Hospitality & Tourism Administration* (The Haworth Press, Inc.) Vol. 1, No. 1, 2000, pp. 71-88; and: *Global Alliances in Tourism and Hospitality Management* (ed: John C. Crotts, Dimitrios Buhalis, and Roger March) The Haworth Press, Inc., 2000, pp. 71-88. Single or multiple copies of this article are available for a fee from The Haworth Document Delivery Service [1-800-342-9678, 9:00 a.m. - 5:00 p.m. (EST). E-mail address: getinfo@haworthpressinc.com].

scales, tourism planners and operators have been discovering the power of collaborative action and are moving away from the adversarial model (Selin 1993, Crotts, Aziz and Raschid 1998). Entrepreneurial partnerships between large and small companies are widely recognised as an important strategy for accelerating growth and innovation (Botkin and Matthews 1992). The purpose of this paper is to investigate "Tastes of Niagara: A Quality Food Alliance," an evolving strategic alliance among the Niagara Region's food producers, processors, distributors, hotels, restaurants, wineries and chefs. In a Region dominated by the image of Niagara Falls, Tastes of Niagara has taken steps to introduce innovative collaborative strategies to promote regional cuisine in Niagara countering criticisms of high leakages often associated with the tourism industry. The paper begins by examining the importance of strategic alliances in the tourism industry and more specifically, the paper moves to an investigation of the literature on the linkages between agriculture and tourism. Much of the existing work on the leakages resulting from the use of imported food has been conducted in developing countries and this case study addresses this apparent gap in the literature. The paper will highlight the evolution of the Tastes of Niagara initiative and the steps that have been introduced to enhance and maintain the food Alliance. The results of qualitative in-depth interviews conducted with participants at all points along the production/consumption chain are presented to get a better understanding of the operating structure of the Alliance. In an era of increasing competitive forces, it is important to document successful cases of collaboration as possible future blueprints for other tourism operators.

STRATEGIC ALLIANCES AND TOURISM

Strategic alliances have been well researched with much of the work conducted at the dyadic level relating to the causes and consequences of partnerships (Gulati 1998). In the current business environment, Magun (1996) argues that firms are faced with three alternate growth strategies: internal expansion and business start-up; acquisitions and mergers; and strategic alliances. In recent years, of the three options, strategic alliances have become increasingly prominent. Gulati (1998, 293) defines strategic alliances as "voluntary arrangements between firms involving exchange, sharing, or co-development of products, technologies, or services. They can occur as a result of a wide range of motives and goals and can take a variety of forms, and can occur across vertical and horizontal boundaries." The more obvious reasons for the rapid development of strategic alliances are related to resource pooling; economies of scale or scope; and cost and risk sharing among alliance partners. Magun (1996) argues, however, that the more subtle, deeper, and permanent driving forces behind the rapid growth of alliances can be attributed to: globalisation of the world economy; acceptance that competition by itself does not necessarily promote optimum innovation-led growth; and the realisation that both competition and co-operation between firms is needed to ensure growth in an uncertain and dynamic world. The need for complementary specialised inputs have forced firms to change their business strategies to create organisational flexibility in value-chain activities such as R&D, distribution channels and strategic alliances (Magun 1996). With respect to tourism, Smith (1993) argues that it is the organisation of the components of the industry (facilities, services and hospitality) which are combined to provide an experience of value for the customer resulting in the overall tourism product. One of the main objectives within the Tastes of Niagara Alliance is to generate a high quality tourism product through a value chain which promotes the use of local agricultural products within the tourism industry.

Within the fragmented tourism industry Selin (1993) argues that communication has largely been underdeveloped. The causes of poor communication have been attributed to geographic and organisational fragmentation; long chain distribution systems; jurisdictional boundaries; ideological differences; centralised government decision-making; competitive rhetoric; pay for representation systems; and emphasis on one-way communication. Despite these barriers, steps have been taken to increase linkages between the sectors. Strategic alliances in the airline industry such as the Star Alliance (Air Canada, Lufthansa, Scandinavian Airlines, Thai Airways, United Airlines and Varig) and in the sectors of travel agents, lodging and information technology (Computer Reservation Systems) illustrate the trend of co-operation emerging in the industry (Go and Williams 1993).

Crotts, Aziz and Rashid (1998) examined the importance of maintaining successful relationships between buyers and sellers in the international travel trade in New Zealand. Similar to research trends in economics incorporating social relations (Grabher 1993), the authors found that commitment is an important element in the buyer-supplier relationship. They found that social bonds, co-operation, trust, communication, performance satisfaction and comparison level of alternatives were statistically related to supplier commitment. The organising committees of Tastes of Niagara Alliance have identified trust, commitment and communication as important components of the Alliance. The following section further sets the framework for the case study by examining previous work on the relationship between food and agriculture and the importance of forming strategic alliances with local suppliers.

FOOD AND TOURISM

The relationship between tourism and agriculture is complex (Telfer and Wall 1996) as the agricultural sector not only provides inputs into the tourism industry, the rural landscape can also evolve into a tourism product. While there is a general recognition that there should be an increased reliance on local resources, studies warn of the leakages that can occur when the tourist industry relies on imported foods (Belisle 1983, Taylor et al. 1991, Wilkinson 1987). Many of the participants in rural tourism are small and have limited budgets and need to work together in order to promote their product. Hjalager (1996) for example found that individual rural tourism providers had marketing difficulties. In some cases rural tourism providers had to opt for marketing channels such as local tourists boards, summer cottage intermediaries or other tourist enterprises with complementary products if there were no colleagues available to work together in joint initiatives.

Models have been developed which illustrate the linkages between the sectors of tourism and agriculture. In a developing country context, Lundgren (1973) proposed an evolutionary three-stage model of entrepreneurial development based on the demands for local food from hotels which hypothesised that, over time, there would be increased reliance on local food. Following an initial stage where a new large metropolitan hotel complex is established with integrated systems that rely on foreign suppliers, a locally based and controlled system evolves. In the intermediate stage, the development of local agricultural wholesaling and marketing firms allows for the involvement of local suppliers. In the advanced stage, local wholesaling is further expanded and leads to the stimulation of agricultural production and hinterland development. The model developed by Bowen, Cox and Fox (1991) outlines the market linkages between the following sectors: external economy; visitors; visitor industry; production of agriculture and agriculturally based services; and resources (natural resources, labour, capital and entrepreneurship). Commenting beyond traditional direct linkages, the authors note that non-market linkages including the aesthetic value of agricultural land as a commodity for tourism are not included. Finally, Telfer (1996) has diagrammed the numerous linkages involved in the purchasing of local agricultural products for large-scale hotels.

As Belisle (1983) suggests, food represents approximately one-third of tourist expenditures and the degree to which the tourist industry relies on imported food can have a significant affect on the social and economic impacts of tourism. Bowen, Cox and Fox (1991) have generalised the reasons for using imported agricultural products as ones of availability, price, consistency and the quality of local products. The barriers to increasing local food production for input into the tourist industry include economic, technological, behavioural, physical and marketing obstacles (Belisle 1983). Telfer and Wall (1996) have suggested that the degree to which local agriculturally related firms have the ability to trade with the tourism industry is related to the scale of enterprises, the interrelationships between entrepreneurs with differing access to resources, and the sizes of enterprises and their associated linkages.

In previous studies (Telfer and Wall 1996, Telfer 1996) it has been demonstrated that large-scale hotels are able to link into existing food distribution channels in developing countries and utilise local agricultural products. The hotels in both studies used existing as well as generating new vertical linkages with the agricultural sector through strategic alliances. The Tastes of Niagara Alliance has attributes of both vertical and horizontal linkages as there is co-operation along and across the value chain. Magun (1996) suggests that the vertical alliance value chain between producers and their suppliers or distributors is focused more on maintaining flexibility and adding value while horizontal alliances are focused more on protecting their core competencies. The paper now turns to investigate the various relationships within The Tastes of Niagara Alliance, an organisation that has important economic and social functions in the community.

THE NIAGARA REGION

The highly urbanised Niagara Region in Southern-Ontario, Canada is an area of contrasts. Noted for Niagara Falls, one of the major tourist attractions in the world, the Region also has historic and cultural centres in Niagara-on-the-Lake, heavy industry in Welland, a regional centre in St Catharines, and an extensive canal and hydroelectric power network (Gayler 1994). While the image of the Region is focused on Niagara Falls, it is also unique in that two Great Lakes (Erie and Ontario), the Niagara River and the Niagara Escarpment border it. The three bodies of water moderate the winters extending the growing season (Shaw 1994). The Niagara Escarpment also assists in airflow preventing cooler pockets of air from settling in low-lying areas. Part of the Niagara Region is known as the Fruit Belt of Canada (Chapman 1994). Being a Temperate Zone, the Region is able to produce a wide range of products including peaches, plums, cherries, grapes, apples, apricots, nectarines, kiwi and a wide range of vegetables. These favourable conditions help form the heart of the local wine industry. The mild winters have also given rise to the largest greenhouse industry in Canada, generating fresh produce year round. In addition, chicken, quail, pork, beef, fresh water fish, ostrich, venison and lamb are all raised in the Region.

The diversity of agricultural practices has led to the development of agritourism in the form of farm and winery tours. The wine industry in Canada has undergone radical changes with the introduction of the North American Free Trade Deal and GATT rulings (Aspler 1995) which has resulted in the development of a cottage wine industry. Baird (1995:84) stated that "Vintners pour endless glasses of sample wines, and many provide lunches and dinners in their restaurants overlooking the vineyard." Wineries and restaurants are taking an active role in the development of a regional cuisine (Duncan 1995). McLaughlin, Roberts and McKay suggest that (1995) Canadians want affordable food produced in an environmentally friendly manner. They also want to take leisurely drives through the countryside where foods are grown to enjoy the hamlets, villages and wood lots. The development of the Wine Route connecting over 27 wineries and Agricultural Adventures (a two-day farm open house of 16 area farms) are indications of the development of rural tourism in the Niagara Region.

EVOLUTION OF THE TASTES OF NIAGARA PROGRAM

The "Tastes of Niagara: A Quality Food Alliance" is a non-profit strategic alliance among food producers, processors, distributors, hotels, restaurants, wineries and chefs in the region. The overriding goal of the organisation is to improve "the social and economic well-being of Niagarans through increasing the visibility and preferential purchase of Niagara agricultural products both within the Region and outside of it" (Vision Niagara 1996, 7). The movement is based on developing a Niagara-based regional cuisine using high quality local products. The program started in 1993 and evolved out of the Agri-Hospitality Committee of Vision Niagara Planning & Development Inc., a non-profit, volunteer organisation. Initially the program was focused on connecting chefs in the region's more expensive restaurants with some of its more unique food products. An initial meeting of chefs, food producers and processors organised by Tastes of Niagara identified the need for increased communication between various groups (Vision Niagara 1996). A series of tours of farms and food processing plants were conducted to introduce chefs to local area products. The purpose of the tours was to provide chefs in the area an opportunity to see first hand the type of products available locally and in some cases how they are processed. The tours provided an opportunity to strengthen economic and social relationships within the organisation. Past regional farm tours have included: a vegetable farm and grain milling operation, a strawberry farm, a cheese processing plant, a greenhouse operation specialising in peppers, tomatoes and cucumbers, a peach farm, a quail farm, a hydroponics operation, and a wild game farm. The program has grown rapidly to include a wide diversity of strategic partners as indicated in Table 1.

In order to meet the overriding goal of improving the social and economic well being of people in the region through the preferential purchasing of Niagara products, the committee set forth the following goals and objectives for the Tastes of Niagara Alliance:

TABLE 1. Partners and Products Involved in Tastes of Niagara Program

Primary Producers of Food Products	Processors of Food Products
• Fruit Producers	• Canned, frozen, dried/dehydrated foods
• Vegetable Producers (Field & Green house)	• Fruit and Vegetable juice
• Herb & Edible Flower Producers	• Grape and Fruit Wine
• Poultry Producers	• Cheese, milk, yoghurt, other dairy
• Red Meat Producers (Beef, Venison, etc.)	• Bakery goods
• Dairy Producers	• Specialty flours
• Fish Producers and Fishermen	• Abattoirs and specialty meats
• Nut Producers	
• Mixed Grain Producers	**Hospitality and Tourism Industry**
• Grape Producers	• Restaurants
• Producers of Organic Food Products	• Hotels and Inns
	• Caterers
Food Distributors	• Hospitality & Tourism Education
• Wholesalers and exporters	• Farm and winery tours
• Retail outlets	• Bed & Breakfast
• Chain and independent grocery stores	
• Dairies	**Other**
• Bakeries	• Consumers (area residents and tourists)
• Butchers	• Food and wine writers
• Farm Markets	• Farm and other equipment suppliers
• Roadside (farm-gate markets)	

Source: Vision Niagara 1996

1. Encouraging and promoting the development of standards of excellence for the production, preparation and sale of Niagara agricultural products.
2. Promoting wide awareness and acceptance of these standards by industry and the public.
3. Raising the profile of those who accept and implement these standards as purveyors of quality foods and as members of the Alliance.
4. Creating greater loyalty to and among members.
5. Creating greater loyalty to Niagara food products.
6. Identifying the members in an annual guide (for tourists and residents) which would preferentially market member establishments.
7. Promotion of the commercial interests of members by the effective marketing of Niagara as: a world class destination and a supplier of quality food products for domestic and export markets.
8. Developing existing and new products and product sources in Niagara.
9. Defining the distinctive nature and quality of Niagara food products. (Vision Niagara 1996)

An official trademark depicting a sunrise over fields and vineyards identifies members who meet local quality and quantity requirements and are dedicated to publicising and promoting the use of high quality Niagara food products within Niagara and abroad. Design of the logo was achieved through a public contest. The Tastes of Niagara program promotes excellence in local agricultural products and services. Members are committed to maintaining *a chain of excellence* from the field to the table. The chain of excellence has six links: the farmer, the processor, the distributor, the chef, the server and finally the consumer. In order to maintain the chain of excellence, members are required to:

1. Preferentially provide to and purchase from other members and the public the highest quality local products at competitive prices to the public
2. Pay for all purchases at agreed times and use products within a time frame that ensures optimum conditions
3. Commit to high standards of quality in products, hospitality, ambience, cleanliness and service
4. Prominently display the Tastes of Niagara logo and certificate of membership at or in their place of business
5. Participate in marketing efforts of the Alliance (Vision Niagara 1996, 11)

A formal structure has been established for membership fees placing businesses into three categories: (1) Producers/Processors/Chefs/Restaurants/Caterers/and other Food Service Organisations; (2) Corporate Members–supportive companies desiring membership; and (3) Affiliate Members–those businesses that provide services to other members, related businesses and educational institutions. Annual memberships are set at $50 CDN for all groups except restaurants which are priced according to number of seats. Other funding comes from sponsorships and brokerage fees for special events. General standards of quality have been established for: Products for Food Service, Mutual Responsiveness and Effective Communication. Food service personnel are educated about the program and indicate to customers the origin of products.

The Alliance has developed a number of initiatives to strengthen the links between agriculture and tourism-related industries. The Agri-Hospitality Resource Guide for Niagara contains a listing of the region's food producers, processors, chefs and restaurants. Table 2 contains a list of the number and types of organisations included in the Guide in 1998. The Guide has been useful to local chefs in identifying sources of high quality local products. It serves producers and processors who are able to use the Guide to expand their customer base. Companies are listed in alphabetical order by the type of product they sell.

The entry for each company includes a contact address, products sold, availability, products that are value added, companies that deliver, and how

TABLE 2. Number of Organisations Involved in Tastes of Niagara

Fruit and Vegetable Growers and Processors	50
Meat and Poultry Producers	22
Fish Producers	4
Dairy Producers and Processors	5
Farm Markets	5
Distributors	3
Other Producers and Processors & Services	10
Wineries	21
Restaurants/Chefs, Caterers and Cooking Schools	<u>23</u>
Total	143

Source: Tastes of Niagara Agri-Hospitality Resource Guide, 1998

companies usually sell their product (retail, wholesale or farm gate). Members of Tastes of Niagara are highlighted. Users of the guide are encouraged to utilise member companies first. The Guide contains the Foodland Ontario Produce Growth Chart identifying harvest times for over 70 fruits and vegetables. Chefs can also telephone the Tastes of Niagara office staffed by the Executive Director and Events Manager to identify a local source for a particular product.

PROMOTING TASTES OF NIAGARA

The program puts efforts into marketing Niagara's local cuisine throughout the year. Chefs and producers work with Niagara wineries to offer food and wine tastings for the public and to produce special events. For example, Tastes of Niagara was responsible for putting on a dinner for an annual conference of the Federal-Provincial and Territorial Ministers of Agriculture. A sample of the 1998 Tastes of Niagara Special Promotions are presented in Table 3.

A newsletter is published which promotes communication among chefs, producers and the public by reporting on tourism and agricultural events. During the summer of 1998, Tastes of Niagara hosted 6 weekends at Chateau des Charmes Wines Ltd., one of many wineries on the Niagara Wine Route, highlighting local foods and wines. The organisation is also moving into the area of brokering for special events. They recently hired a full-time special event co-ordinator. The Alliance helps arrange food for conferences and seminars by approaching various producers and chefs to work together to organise events. The Alliance has a policy of rotating the honours between member producers and chefs so that various companies receive publicity. The local cable television station has become a source for promotion with Tastes

TABLE 3. Selected Tastes of Niagara 1998 Special Events and Promotions

---

March
Toronto Wine and Cheese Show
10 area chefs using Niagara's produce perform cooking demonstrations

May
Tastes of Niagara team with Heart Niagara to provide a lunch using
Niagara produce for 600 participants in the Bloom Festival Road Race

June
Tastes of Niagara, Strewn Winery and Cuisine Canada present an evening
highlighting Niagara Producers and Growers

July
Tastes of Niagara prepares a Showcase at Fort George for the Provincial
and Federal Ministers of Agriculture from across Canada, Chefs, wineries
and growers participate

Chateau des Charmes (winery), Niagara College Maid of the Mist Centre
(chef school) and Tastes of Niagara partner for six weekends in July and
August to offer food and wine

August
Fourth Annual Showcase
Chefs, wineries, growers and food producers join to promote Niagara
cuisine to an expected sell-out of over 800 guests.

Source: Tastes of Niagara Agri-Hospitality Resource Guide, 1998

of Niagara chefs regularly appearing to showcase local wines and related products. The organisation has made special appearances in food and wine trade shows in Canada and abroad.

One measure of success for the organisation has been the yearly growth in the Annual Show Case held every August. The 4th and most recent Annual Showcase represented twenty-two restaurants and twenty wineries. A sell-out crowd of over 800 attended. Chefs prepared sample dishes using products from the Niagara Region. The event has grown from 120 visitors at the first Showcase to predictions for over 1,000 visitors for 1999. The cost of the evening is $45 CDN which allows the visitors to sample as much food as they want. They are provided with a complimentary glass of wine in a souvenir glass and tickets are sold for additional wine samples (Benner 1998). The organisation now boasts five community corporate partners and fourteen sponsors for this event.

The organisation is preparing two additional projects that are more ambitious. The first is the Niagara Food Products Information and Distribution Centre. Plans are to be phased in over time once funding can be secured. The local Distribution Centre will act as a clearing-house where producers drop off products to be stored in refrigerated units for purchase. The Distribution centre will be responsible for co-ordinating information between producers and buyers as to product availability and demand. The purpose of this project is to develop a local method for purchasing local products. Currently, many products are shipped out of the region to Toronto to large markets and later returned by distributors to Niagara. Tastes of Niagara staff would like to see the Distribution Centre developed into a stand alone independent business.

The second major project is entitled "Niagara's Taste of the Month." This program is designed to produce, promote, and market Niagara food products in quantities and packages that can be delivered or shipped as gifts and promotional items. Each month, a different product or combination of products will be assembled to represent "Niagara's Taste of the Month." The program will increase awareness of the quality and diversity of products available in Niagara. The project is to become a free-standing business under a license from Vision Niagara. The target markets for the product include visitors to the region as well as businesses who are seeking promotional, incentive and gift items. Advertising outlets will include wineries, food outlets, restaurants, members of Tastes of Niagara, and various media outlets. While these major projects have yet to fully materialise, both will rely heavily on the co-operation of all Alliance members to succeed.

METHODOLOGY

To further investigate the linkages between the sectors involved in Tastes of Niagara, 38 qualitative interviews were completed with producers, processors, restaurant operators, chefs, wineries and members of the organising committee (20 producers, 14 chefs, 4 wineries). Both the 1998 Tastes of Niagara Annual Board Meeting and the Annual Tastes of Niagara Showcase were attended where current issues and concerns were discussed. Producers and processors were interviewed while the researcher participated in Rural Routes: An Agricultural Adventure. This two day event (August 22-23, 1998) involves 16 area farms and related agricultural businesses open to the public for free farm tours. Hosts of the tour included: a wild game farm, a herb farm, a quail farm, greenhouses, livestock operations, and a grower's demonstration farm. Respondents interviewed were asked to discuss the nature of agritourism and the links between tourism and agriculture. Supplementary questions were asked and respondents were asked to explain their answers. They were also asked for comments and suggestions on the initiative and strengthening ties between sectors. As Veal (1997) indicated, qualitative in-depth interviews are less structured than a questionnaire based interview and every interview in a research study, although dealing with the same issues, will be different. As a result, at this stage in the research, statistical analysis is not performed. The results of this preliminary investigation will serve as the foundation for more detailed future research. The following sections outline the main findings from the interviews.

FINDINGS

The broader concept of agritourism, the Alliance, and efforts to continue to improve and strengthen them enjoy wide support in the community. While there were differences between all respondents as to what constitutes agritourism, there is a concern that there needs to be a lasting link which will inform the local entrepreneurs of the potential contribution that agriculture can make towards tourism. All of the farms visited stressed the importance of introducing products to the tourists and educating them as to how the crops are grown and harvested. One of the producers felt that a governing body, possibly with municipal assistance, should inventory all agritourism establishments and events and provide training workshops and seminars for local farmers wanting to become involved in agritourism. In terms of communication, the Agri-Hospitality Guide has proved to be a useful tool according to the chefs for identifying sources of local products and has helped link together a very diverse group of industries.

The Tastes of Niagara organisation has proven to be a key strategic alliance for those involved and the opportunity to work co-operatively has raised the profile of regional cuisine in Niagara. Niagara cuisine has also recently been featured in Maclean's, a Canadian weekly newsmagazine. Further documenting the continuing evolution of food, wine and tourism, Vineland Estates Winery is planning to open an international culinary institute with lodging for 70 students, visiting chefs and agritourists (Chidley 1998). A proposal discovered during the interviews would see the construction of a Farmers Market to serve year-round to promote Niagara's farms, wineries and horticultural industries. It would direct visitors to farm tours, pick-your-own orchards, B&Bs, local restaurants and events. The controversy with the project, however, is that the location for the proposed centre is on prime agricultural land.

All of the respondents viewed the promotion and development of communication between members and consumers as the main task for the Alliance. Members wanted the Alliance to take steps to increase communication with the public and generate new marketing initiatives. The need to work together was clearly reflected in the informal interviews with farmers who all indicated they have limited funding for independent marketing which is similar to the findings of Hjalager (1996). Tastes of Niagara staff is viewed as a sounding board for the Alliance. Those interviewed felt the staff should continue to have a strong administrative role with the development of the newsletter, special events, and the Agri-Hospitality Guide.

Suggestions for improvement centred on increasing communication between farmers and local restaurants. One comment was made that all members need to be viewed as being part of the same community. Respondents proposed several mini-alliances between wineries, educational institutions, hotels and restaurants. "Elegant Traditions" is one such scheme which currently links a local festival theatre with B&Bs and a winery. There was also a suggestion for increased joint marketing efforts between local wineries and wineries in upstate New York. A desire to draw tourists to the agritourism sites throughout the year was expressed. There is a need to gather better data on who is visiting the various establishments. Some suggested an increase in the number of tours of farms with B&Bs.

Interviews revealed a number of initiatives to further illustrate expanding linkages within the Alliance. A quail farm joined forces with two different restaurants at the Annual Showcase. Four wineries, the Vintners Quality Alliance and the Pork Provincial Marketing Board partnered in preparation for the Niagara Grape and Wine Festival. Each of the four wineries along with area chefs created four recipes using pork paired with local wines which were served at the Showcase. The group has produced a brochure detailing the partnership and recipes offered. One new winery has opened a cooking school and displayed wines and dishes at the Showcase prepared at their school. To promote links in the local community, the cooking school recently invited local B&B operators to a free cooking demonstration.

Several concerns were also raised by respondents surrounding agritourism and the Tastes of Niagara initiative. The Niagara Region is highly urbanised and development is putting pressure on prime agricultural land. One of the respondents indicated the need for a study on the impacts of tourism in the region and its relation to agriculture. Concern was raised over the development of new restaurants at wineries. As boutique wineries continue to develop there is a natural extension to open restaurants on site. Two of the restaurants interviewed indicated they have already been serving and promoting local wines. With the wineries opening restaurants in addition to their wine shops, there is worry that some of the established restaurants may lose customers to the wineries. One of the wineries on the other hand was worried that there may be an over development of wineries causing over supply. These concerns echo statements of Magun (1996) indicating that those involved in horizontal alliances are concerned about protecting core competencies.

One of the small independent farmers expressed concern over the prices they received from the market-place and how little control they often have.

The smaller farmer was worried about competition from larger farms and the strength of larger wineries on grape prices. One respondent cautioned about the danger of farms becoming too commercialised and losing their authenticity. Another farmer expressed concerns that the high tourist season occurs during the farms' busiest period, raising issues of liability.

One of the main difficulties facing Tastes of Niagara is a lack of funding. There is hesitation to raise membership fees as the program is relatively new. However, the lack of funding is preventing involvement in a wider range of activities such as the Distribution Centre and Tastes of the Month. The development of the Distribution Centre would require a substantial financial commitment by individuals and companies. The new firm would need a cold storage facility and it must have the ability to co-ordinate daily shipments varying in size by season.

One of the goals of the Alliance is to determine the types of information required by all parties if the organisation is to move towards establishing the Distribution Centre (Auld 1998). Responses of members indicate the complexity within the Alliance and reflect on the larger complexity of the relationship between tourism and agriculture. Growers, producers and processors would need to know chefs' and consumers' needs, demographics of surrounding areas, trends in society, new farming techniques, availability of new technology, government's product standards, distribution systems, and quality control. Chefs and restaurants would need to know seasonal availability of local, regional and imported products. They require names and locations of local processors, how the products are produced (green-house, hydroponics, pesticide use), quality control methods, distribution system, pricing and payment requirements, and finally, involvement in special events. Information required by the public to help promote the entire concept includes: product variety and availability, growing practices, retail and farm gate information, location of rural routes, location of wineries, and information on upcoming events, and relevant Internet addresses (Auld 1998).

DISCUSSION AND CONCLUSIONS

The development and maintenance of horizontal and vertical strategic alliances is becoming critical for both the tourism and agricultural sectors for businesses to be competitive. The tourism industry is diverse and relies on many industries to successfully deliver a high quality product to the consumer. The relationship between tourism and agriculture is complex and food and wine have also become tourist attractions. A review of Tastes of Niagara has shown it possible to overcome many of the barriers that exist between industries to form lasting partnerships within a community. As indicated by Chidley (1998), it is important that in the establishment of regional cuisine all parties work together. As the strategic alliance of Tastes of Niagara has illustrated, partnerships can evolve and become stronger and broader in scope. What started as a desire by chefs to use local products has evolved into a large organisation committed to promoting local cuisine. Similar to the evolutionary model of Lundgren (1973) alliances between agriculture and tourism grow and evolve. The Alliance maintains a quality product through a value chain starting in the field and ending with the customer.

There are strict guidelines for members dictating the use of local products and giving recognition to area producers. Alliance members take part in joint marketing campaigns, creating special events, developing linkages with local producers, creating new partnerships, and developing new products. An important element in the success or failure of programs is funding and the Alliance relies on corporate sponsorship and special events to generate money in addition to membership fees. Opportunities also exist to partner with governmental agencies associated with tourism and agriculture.

Benefits associated with strong alliances are many. Restaurants use high quality local products helping to develop regional cuisine. If quality and quantity can not be maintained, import substitution may occur. Access to high quality food benefits the customer as well as the farmers as they may have new markets in which to sell their products. Use of local food in the restaurants can be used as a marketing technique to attract customers and it also presents them as a good community citizen. The tourism industry is often criticised for having high leakages and limited connections to the surrounding community. By establishing linkages with local food and beverage suppliers the local multiplier effect may increase thereby increasing the positive economic impact of the tourism industry. Once tourists have been exposed to various regional foods and wines, they may also wish to purchase these local products thereby further stimulating the agricultural sector.

The formation of Tastes on Niagara has generated new products. The organisation is now involved in brokering for special events to further highlight the products of Niagara. Participating businesses are receiving increased recognition in the local community and abroad Chefs and wine makers are taking products to international trade shows. There, joint marketing efforts are particularly important for the smaller firms that are unable to undertake large scale marketing initiatives.

Difficulties arise in developing strategic alliance between the tourism and agricultural sectors. It takes a great deal of effort and time to develop lasting economic and social relationships. However, the Alliance is growing and the public is becoming more interested in regional cuisine. Difficulties outlined above in developing the Niagara Distribution Centre are characteristic of the problems similar alliances would encounter. Utilising local agricultural products raises issues of seasonality for both products and the number of tourists.

Restaurants change menus and local farmers need to be prepared to meet demands of small orders frequently. The difficulty of linking small producers with the tourism industry presents challenges associated with scale of operation and reliability (Telfer and Wall 1996). Hotels and restaurants may find it cheaper and more convenient to purchase imported products rather than spending time to seek out local sources. Even with the success of Tastes of Niagara, some of the participants want to create even stronger links between members. Vertical linkages within agritourism are concerned with strengthening ties, however, those involved in horizontal linkages are concerned about potential increased competition within the Alliance. Without consultation and careful development plans, conflicts could develop. Development of restaurants at wineries is raising some concern. Fund raising for the Alliance's special events and marketing programs is difficult, making the use of sponsorships and governmental assistance critical.

Much of the work focusing on leakages resulting from the use of imported goods has been written in a developing country context. Facing uncertainty over the quality and quantity of supply, many establishments are forced to import products generating high level of leakages (Belisle 1983, Taylor et al. 1991, Wilkinson 1987). In a developed country context where highly complex distribution systems exist, leakages may also result as it may be easier and cheaper to purchase imported food. In the case of Niagara, much of the local produce is shipped out of the region to the larger markets in Toronto before it is later returned to Niagara by distributors. The Tastes of Niagara Alliance has illustrated that with a high level of commitment from members, steps can be introduced to increase the direct reliance on local food and thereby reduce the high level of leakages often associated with the tourism industry. Similar to the findings of Telfer (1996) and Telfer and Wall (1996) in a developing country context, this study has shown that if vertical linkages are to be developed and maintained between tourism and agriculture a high level of commitment is required by all of those involved.

At a broader level, the focus of much of the work on alliances in the tourism industry has often been on larger companies such as airlines, travel agencies, lodging companies or in the areas of information technology ignoring the alliances between smaller firms. Food represents an important component of the tourist experience and this paper has illustrated that strategic alliances between businesses involved in the production and distribution of local agricultural products can be an important component in the delivery of a high quality tourist experience. This paper also presents a number of future research questions relating to the long-term management of voluntary strategic alliances. Smaller firms wanting to remain competitive and innovative need to carefully examine the value of strategic alliances within the tourism delivery system.

BIBLIOGRAPHY

Auld, S. (1998). *Distribution Centre Survey Results.* Unpublished document.

Aspler, T. (1995). *Tony Aspler's Vintage Canada Second Edition.* Toronto: McGraw-Hill Ryerson Limited.

Baird, E. (1995). The Future of Ontario's Fruit Industry. In J.M. Powers & A. Stewart (Eds.) *Northern Bounty A Celebration of Canadian Cuisine.* (pp. 79-84). Toronto: Random House of Canada.

Benner, A. (1998, August 24). Niagara's home-grown taste celebrated. *The Standard.* pp. B2.

Belisle, F. J. (1983). Tourism and Food Production in the Caribbean. *Annals of Tourism Research.* 10 (4) 497-513.

Botkin, J. W. & Matthews, J. B. (1992). *Winning Combinations The Coming Wave of Entrepreneurial Partnerships Between Large and Small Companies.* Toronto: John Wiley & Sons, Inc.

Bowen, R., Cox, L. and Fox, F. (1991). The Interface Between Tourism and Agriculture. *Journal of Tourism Studies.* 2 (2) 43-54.

Chapman, P. (1994). Agriculture in Niagara: An Overview. In H. Gayler (Ed.) *Niagara's Changing Landscapes.* (pp. 279-300). Ottawa: Carleton University Press.

Chidley, J. (1998). Haute Canuck. *Maclean's.* 111 (34) 36-40.

Crotts, J., Aziz, A. & Raschid, A. (1998). Antecedents of supplier's commitment to wholesale buyers in the international travel trade. *Tourism Management.* 19 (2) 127-134.

Duncan, D. (1995). Ontario Cooking: Cuisines in Transition. In J. M. Powers & A. Stewart (Eds.) *Northern Bounty A Celebration of Canadian Cuisine.* (pp. 102-112). Toronto: Random House of Canada.

Gayler, H. J. (1994). Urban Development and Planning in Niagara. In H. Gayler (Ed.) *Niagara's Changing Landscapes.* (pp. 241-278). Ottawa: Carleton University Press.

Go, F. M., & Williams, A. P. (1993). Competing and Cooperating in the Changing Tourism Channel System. *Journal of Travel & Tourism Marketing.* 2 (2/3) 229-248.

Grabher, G. (1993). Rediscovering the social in the economics of interfirm relations. in G. Grabher (Ed.), (pp. 1-33). *The embedded firm, On the socioeconomics of industrial networks.* London: Routledge.

Gulati, R. (1998). Alliances and Networks. *Strategic Management Journal.* 19 293-317.

Hjalager, A. (1996). Agricultural diversification into tourism: evidence of a European community development program. *Tourism Management.* 17 (2) 103-111.

Lundgren, J. O. (1973). Tourism impact/island entrepreneurship in the Caribbean. Paper presented to the Conference of Latin American Geographers. In Mathieson, A. and Wall, G. (1982) *Tourism: Economic, Physical and Social Impacts.* London: Longman.

McLaughlin, R., Roberts, O. & McKay, S. (1995). A Vision for Agriculture. In J. M. Powers and A. Stewart (Eds.) *Northern Bounty A Celebration of Canadian Cuisine.* (pp. 95-101). Toronto: Random House of Canada.

Magun, S. (1996). *The Development of Strategic Alliances in Canadian Industries: A Micro Analysis.* Working Paper Number 13, Industry Canada.

Selin, S. (1993). Collaborative Alliances: New Interorganizational Forms in Tourism. *Journal of Travel & Tourism Marketing. 2* (2/3) 217-227.

Shaw, T. B. (1994). Climate of the Niagara Region. In H. Gayler (Ed.) *Niagara's Changing Landscapes.* (pp. 111-137). Ottawa: Carleton University Press.

Smith, S. (1993). The Tourist Product. *Annals of Tourism Research. 21* (3) 582-595.

Tastes of Niagara Agri-Hospitality Resource Guide, 1998. Tastes of Niagara.

Taylor, B. E., J. B. Morison and E. M. Fleming. (1991). The Economic Impact of Food Import Substitution in the Bahamas. *Social and Economic Studies. 40* (2) 45-62.

Telfer, D. J. & Wall, G. (1996). Linkages Between Tourism and Food Production. *Annals of Tourism Research. 23* (3) 635-653.

Telfer, D. J. (1996). Food Purchases in a Five Star Hotel: A Study of the Aquilla Prambanan Hotel, Yogyakarta Indonesia. *Tourism Economics, The Business and Finance of Tourism and Recreation. 2* (4) 321-337.

Veal, A.J. (1997). *Research Methods for Leisure and Tourism, A Practical Guide 2nd Edition.* London: Pitman Publishing.

Vision Niagara. (1996). *Tastes of Niagara: A Quality Food Alliance Handbook.* Vision Niagara Planning and Development Inc.

Wilkinson, P. F. (1987). Tourism in Small Island Nations: A Fragile Dependence. *Leisure Studies. 6* (2) 128-146.

Theoretical Perspectives Applied to Inter-Organisational Collaboration on Britain's Inland Waterways

Alan Fyall
Ben Oakley
Annette Weiss

SUMMARY. The increasing need to forge partnerships to accomplish collective and organisational goals in tourism has been theorized at length in recent literature. However, limited research has been published to apply such ideas to existing collaborative forms. Within the context of inland waterway boating holidays in Britain this paper explores the inter-organisational behaviour of a contemporary case, the inland *Waterways* consortium, an initiative led by the British Tourist

Alan Fyall is Lecturer in Marketing at Napier University, Edinburgh, Scotland. His research interests are primarily in sustainable tourism, heritage tourism management and tourism marketing alliances.

Ben Oakley is Lecturer in Tourism and Marketing at Southampton Business School, Southampton, England. His research spans national lottery millennium projects in the United Kingdom.

Annette Weiss is Lecturer in Tourism and Marketing at Southampton Business School, Southampton, England. She has particular interest in water-based tourism initiatives.

Address correspondence to: Alan Fyall, Lecturer in Marketing, Marketing Cognate Group, Napier University Business School, South Craig, Craighouse Campus, Craighouse Road, Edinburgh, EH10 5LG, Scotland (e-mail: a.fyall@napier.ac.uk).

The authors wish to express thanks to Gerald Vinten, Professor John Latham and Ashok Ranchhod for their comments on an earlier version of this article. Any errors that remain are solely the responsibility of the authors.

[Haworth co-indexing entry note]: "Theoretical Perspectives Applied to Inter-Organisational Collaboration on Britain's Inland Waterways." Fyall, Alan, Ben Oakley, and Annette Weiss. Co-published simultaneously in *International Journal of Hospitality & Tourism Administration* (The Haworth Press, Inc.) Vol. 1, No. 1, 2000, pp. 89-112; and: *Global Alliances in Tourism and Hospitality Management* (ed: John C. Crotts, Dimitrios Buhalis, and Roger March) The Haworth Press, Inc., 2000, pp. 89-112. Single or multiple copies of this article are available for a fee from The Haworth Document Delivery Service [1-800-342-9678, 9:00 a.m. - 5:00 p.m. (EST). E-mail address: getinfo@haworthpressinc.com].

Authority. The paper considers the findings of a series of in-depth interviews and survey work with members of the inland *Waterways* consortium, which is comprised of local authorities, government agencies, and private firms. Theoretical contributions from the literature are used throughout to identify predictive possibilities and advance existing knowledge of the internal dynamics of an inter-organisational collaborative tourism initiative. The first half of the paper compares theoretical perspectives on the origin and development of collaborative action to the genesis and development of the *Waterways* case. The second half of the paper addresses the inter-organisational dynamics and structure of the inland *Waterways* consortium with consideration of the future potential of this new collaborative entity. The paper concludes with a set of specific recommendations for the consortium as well as offering general directions for future research. *[Article copies available for a fee from The Haworth Document Delivery Service: 1-800-342-9678. E-mail address: getinfo@haworthpressinc.com <Website: http://www.haworthpressinc.com>]*

KEYWORDS. Inter-organisational collaboration, co-operative marketing alliances, tourism partnerships, inland waterway boating holidays

INTRODUCTION

The increasing use of collaboration to meet collective and organisational goals in tourism has been discussed at length in recent years (Gunn, 1994; Long, 1996; 1997; Turner, 1992). The multisectoral and interdependent nature of tourism clearly serves as the catalytic focus for the propagation of more extensive co-ordination and collective decision making throughout the entire industry (Inskeep, 1991). Rapid economic, social and political change also provide powerful incentives for tourism organisations to concede their independence and to participate in joint-decision making (Murphy, 1985; Smith, 1991; Witt & Moutinho, 1989). Osborne and Gaebler (1992) add that the increasingly nebulous partition between government and business serves as a key stimulus for collaborative activity; budgetary constraints, combined with political and public pressure for greater accountability, proving to be particular engines for collaborative tourism initiatives. Whatever the specific type of initiative in question, Gray and Wood (1991) contend that organisations are finding it advantageous, and often necessary, to find partners to work towards mutually desirable ends. Selin (1993) adds that whether one refers to such initiatives as tourism partnerships, tourism coalitions or co-operative tourism marketing alliances, collaboration signifies the common ground between them all. Gray's (1989:227) seminal definition of collaboration as 'a process of joint-decision making among key stakeholders of a problem domain about the future of that domain' is of particular pertinence here.

This paper reviews this and other literature to provide the theoretical framework for a study into the origin, development and collaborative dynamics of the inland *Waterways* consortium, an initiative led by the British Tourist Authority (BTA). The inland *Waterways* consortium is a collaborative initiative which is seeking to more effectively promote inland waterway boating holidays in Britain and Ireland to the lucrative international market. The first half of the paper compares the existing literature on the origin and development of collaborative action to the genesis and evolution of the *Waterways* case. The second half of the paper addresses a number of theoretical perspectives and applies them to the inter-organisational dynamics and structure of the inland *Waterways* consortium. The paper concludes with specific recommendations for the consortium as well as offering general directions for future research.

INTER-ORGANISATIONAL COLLABORATION

Interest in inter-organisational collaboration in tourism has arisen at a time of increasing environmental turbulence and operational complexity for organisations of all kinds. The need to forge strategic alliances has been recognised by organisational theorists and practitioners alike and has focused increasing attention on issues of partnership, coalition, co-operation and collaboration in dynamic environments (Long, 1996; Selin, 1993). However, despite the palpable environmental pressures, the competitive nature of tourism, particularly at the local level, has not always contributed to an easy and trusting alliance in tourism marketing and management schemes (Holder, 1992). The underdeveloped nature of many tourism communication systems, the enduring geographic and organisational fragmentation within the tourism industry, jurisdictional boundaries and ideological disputes, primarily between public and private sector organisations, often constrain the effective adoption and implementation of collaborative tourism initiatives (Selin, 1993).

However, collaboration is now widespread in the funding of many public tourism initiatives in Britain with urban regeneration and national lottery schemes, amongst others, demanding 'partnerships' as a precondition of finance. Indeed, Palmer (1996) argues that collaboration allows a bridge to be developed between the bureaucratic production culture of local government and the marketing culture adopted by the private tourism sector. Palmer (1996) goes further to suggest that the lack of a marketing culture in many local authority departments has motivated numerous alliances with private sector organisations to exchange core competencies. The private sector generally has a much greater commitment to a marketing orientation which it can exchange for access to local authority political and economic resources which cannot be obtained on the open market (Waddock, 1989). Cultural differences apart, the contribution of public-private sector collaboration to the development of tourism remains unchallenged (Boivin, 1987; Crompton, 1990; Gill & Williams, 1994; Gunn, 1994; McGinnis, 1992; Oaks, 1992; Ritchie, 1993; Stevens, 1988). However, despite this, limited research has been published to explain the processes that occur when collaboration takes place (Selin & Chavez, 1995). Long (1996) claims that there is a clear lack of studies that employ theoretical frameworks and method associated with the analysis of inter-organisational collaboration in tourism. Pearce (1992) goes further to suggest that comparatively little research has been conducted on tourist organisations *per se*. Whether in the tourism or organisation literature, questions directed at co-ordination and inter-organisational interaction are especially critical to the analysis of tourist organisations. Jamal and Getz (1995) add that in view of the interdependencies and the simultaneous use of competitive and collaborative strategies in tourism planning, the various stages and actual implementation of the collaboration process require investigation. In turn, Gray and Wood (1991) contend that the focus of theorising needs to shift from the individual organisation to the inter-organisational domain, that is the configuration of organisations linked to a particular problem. The above arguments provide ample evidence to suggest that there is considerable scope to extend the application of theories of inter-organisational collaboration to specific tourism collaborative initiatives.

RESEARCH METHOD

The case study research reported here was motivated by the relative absence of literature which integrates the key themes and theories of inter-organisational collaboration. In particular, how do such theories relate to a current and evolving problem domain and what predictive possibilities do they demonstrate? Work by Gray (1985; 1989), Gray and Wood (1991), Wood and Gray (1991), Jamal and Getz (1995) and Palmer and Bejou (1995) provide much of the theoretical underpinning for the concept of inter-organisational collaboration, whereas more recent work by Long (1997) and Palmer (1998) afford clarification between the degrees of interaction among interest groups involved in tourism development and the governance style of marketing groupings.

The detailed knowledge of the *Waterways* case stems from previous market research conducted by the authors, on behalf of the BTA, entitled *Waterfront and Waterways: Overseas Visitor Research 1997*, which was carried out between May and December 1997. The principal aims of the inland water-ways component of the research were to:

- identify the size and nature of the existing inland waterway boating hol-iday market in terms of overseas visitor bookings value, volume and profile,
- evaluate the ancillary tourism spending and economic impact in rela-tion to inland markets,
- provide some preliminary indication of overseas awareness of the *Wa-terways* Britain and Ireland promotional campaign.

The market research involved the surveying of overseas tourists across Britain and Ireland. The survey methods included self-completion question-naires in three languages, face-to-face interviews conducted in English and volume questionnaires for the marina/boatyard operators. For both the ques-tionnaires and the face-to-face interviews, samples were selected on the basis of boatyard operator location, size of venture, visitor numbers and expert opinion from key industry players to ensure representatives (Edwards et al., 1998).

Although it is not the purpose of this paper to report the findings derived from the above research, the findings do provide much of the contextual background. Further in-depth interviews were undertaken for the purposes of this paper between September 1997 and April 1998. These were semi-struc-tured in nature and were undertaken with the individuals responsible for *Waterways* consortia liaison in four organisations, namely; British Waterways (a government agency responsible for the majority of the inland waterways network), the British Tourist Authority (the national tourist organisation), the Environment Agency (a government agency responsible for most rivers and many inland waterways) and the TMS Partnership (the consortium manage-ment agent). Interviews were normally held at the organisation's premises and recorded on the condition that confidentiality be maintained. The pur-pose of these interviews was to investigate the genesis and development of the *Waterways* consortium from the perspective of the organisation con-cerned. A 'non-directive approach' was used to probe the dynamics and workings of the consortium (Oppenheim, 1992). The information from these sessions provided further contextual background to the previous market re-search. Not all interview respondents had entirely the same perspectives on the dynamics of the consortium. The approach taken is to report findings where the majority of the interviewees reached broad agreement on issues raised. The authors acknowledge the potential for interviewer and respondent bias. However, further interviews conducted over various stages of the con-sortium's existence were not possible on this occasion due to the relative youth of the collaborative entity.

The following section outlines the background to the case before the first main issue, the origin and development of the consortium, is discussed in relation to the literature. The second half of the paper then considers the theoretical perspectives on the inter-organisational dynamics and structure of the inland *Waterways* consortium.

BACKGROUND

Britain, with 2,000 miles of nineteenth century canals and rivers and a stock of 3,500 hire boats managed by around 200 separate hire-boat operators, offers numerous opportunities for inland waterway boating holidays (Hoseason, 1990). Predominately free of commercial traffic, the *inland* waterways of Britain and Ireland's main appeals to overseas visitors are: the opportunity to enjoy the scenery and countryside; a chance to relax and enjoy the peace and quiet; the novelty and nostalgia associated with the entire experience; and the overall reputation of the product (Edwards et al., 1998).

> The friendliness of lock keepers and canal boat people in general is a key factor for most overseas visitors. However, the actual boat remains the main focus for most people. The whole purpose of the holiday is to be able to take things as they come and be spontaneous according to mood and weather. (Boatyard Operator cited in Edwards et al., 1998)

Ad hoc promotional efforts over the past decade have elevated the importance of the overseas tourist to the inland waterways of Britain and Ireland. For example, the overseas market has doubled since 1982 with the proportion of parties made up entirely of foreign visitors increasing from 5% to 15% over the same time period (Edwards et al., 1998). Hence, it would appear that with domestic demand static or slowly declining any significant growth is likely to be generated from overseas.

Although fleet sizes vary, the market is dominated by those operators who have in excess of 200 boats for hire. Hoseasons and Blakes Holidays together account for roughly half of the entire market. These two main companies along with two medium sized operators account for approximately 80% of overseas tourists to Britain and Ireland's inland waterways. However, despite the fact that the majority of overseas boat weeks are sold by the larger operators, many smaller operators continue to register more than a passing interest in the overseas market; valued at £19.3 million for Britain alone in 1997 (Edwards et al., 1998).

The markets which generate the largest numbers of overseas visitors are Germany, the USA and the Scandinavian countries. Not only do overseas visitors tend to stay longer on the water, they also demonstrate a propensity to stay in Britain and/or Ireland for well over two weeks in total. This represents a substantial economic contribution to the domestic tourism economy of both Britain and Ireland and one that has warranted particular marketing attention.

ORIGIN AND DEVELOPMENT
OF THE INLAND WATERWAYS CONSORTIUM

Numerous reasons have been posited to explain the origins of collaborative action (Anderson & Narus, 1990; Macneil, 1974; 1980; Pfeffer & Salanciek, 1978; Reve, 1992; Stern & Reve, 1990; and Williamson, 1975). More recently, Long (1997) identified five common features which specifically underpin the establishment of collaborative initiatives in tourism, notably:

- central government policy to extend private sector involvement in local regional planning and development activity,
- the associated erosion of local government powers and resources and an increased recognition from local government of the necessity and value of partnerships with other agencies,
- the increasing significance of European Union (EU) funded programmes and projects which commonly require a partnership approach,
- the catalytic role of the national tourist boards during the 1980s and 1990s in the formulation of partnership arrangements and the more recent reduction in their resources for this purpose,
- the emergence of the concept of sustainable tourism including the notion of involving 'stakeholders' in the development process.

In the case of inland waterway boating holidays, against a backdrop of geographic and organisational fragmentation coupled with a sector dominated by a small number of large hire-boat operators, the overwhelming desire to compete more effectively overseas provides the driving force for a number of interested parties to join together and establish some form of collaborative initiative. This is consistent with three key pre-conditions proposed in the literature that help stimulate collaborative processes in the initial stages;

- the existence of a turbulent environment (Trist, 1977),
- a set of stakeholders that are joined by a common sense of purpose (Gray, 1985:912),
- an immature infrastructure and underdeveloped systems (Brown, 1980).

In addition to the above, the new initiative reflected a mix between the exchange perspective of inter-organisational relationships proposed by Levine and White (1961) and the resource-dependent approach suggested by Pfeffer and Salanick (1978); the mutual benefits to be gained from collaboration sitting comfortably alongside the need to make the most of scarce resources (Schmidt & Kochan, 1977). Launched in 1996, the inland *Waterways* consortium represents a collaborative initiative between 67 local authorities, 5 of the largest commercial hire-boat operators and 9 trade and government organisations with the endorsement of one major airline, Virgin Atlantic (see Table 1).

As with a number of other collaborative initiatives, the genesis of the inland *Waterways* consortium owes its formation partly to earlier forms of collaborative activity. For example, the 'Great British Cities' group, formed in 1984, was established from an amalgam of major British cities keen to develop their potential as short-break destinations in the domestic market (Page, 1995). This form of collective 'place marketing' by local government

TABLE 1. Membership of the Inland *Waterways* Consortium 1997

MEMBERSHIP CATEGORIES	CONSORTIUM MEMBERS	FINANCIAL CONTRIBUTION (%)
Local Authorities	67 different Local Government Authorities	57%
Commercial Hire- Boat Operators	Hoseasons Holidays Blakes Holidays* Anglo Welsh Waterway Holidays* Alvechurch Boat Centres UK Waterway Holidays	19%
Trade/Government Organisations	*National Tourist Boards* British Tourist Authority* Irish Tourist Board Northern Ireland Tourist Board Wales Tourist Board Scottish Tourist Board *Government Agencies* British Waterways* Environment Agency* *Trade Organisations* British Marine Industries Federation (BMIF)* Association of Professional Cruising Operators (APCO)	13% 8% 3%
EU Regional Development Fund Support	Birmingham Staffordshire	Uncertain

* Steering Group Members

evidently served as the stimulus for a number of British coastal towns who, in 1989, recognised the considerable potential for developing water-based coastal tourism. Key public-sector employees in locations such as Torquay and Poole drove the idea forward and, recognising the potential of the overseas market, sought the involvement of the BTA. The BTA, in turn, undertook to lead a coastal *Waterfront* initiative and quickly established membership and promotional goals which led to the launch of an annual brochure and programme of overseas promotional activity.

The collective success of the coastal *Waterfront* consortium demonstrated to a broader audience the ability and willingness of both the private and public sector to support, and share, the benefits of joint-marketing activity. In 1993, two of Britain's leading inland waterway hire-boat operators, Hoseasons and Blakes, in conjunction with British Waterways, a government agency, lobbied for and funded the inclusion of inland pages in the coastal *Waterfront* brochure. With an increasing commitment to more refined and clearly targeted market segmentation strategies, the BTA launched a diverse range of promotional activity. However, as a consequence of resource constraints at the BTA a decision was made in 1994 to contract out the management and day-to-day operation of the coastal *Waterfront* initiative which, in reality, had made limited progress from its initial objectives. A fixed management fee was agreed with the TMS Partnership, based in Poole, in conjunction with a set of agreed targets. Hence, largely as a consequence of the change in management and the interest generated among inland waterway organisations, a dedicated inland *Waterways* brochure was established in 1996.

To further explore the benefits and drawbacks of collaboration, and underpinning conditions which facilitate the establishment of collaborative initiatives such as the inland *Waterways* consortium, a number of authors postulate a series of common benefits, drawbacks and common characteristics of collaboration. These are summarised in Table 2.

Although not all the benefits and drawbacks identified in Table 2 can be specifically applied to the *Waterways* case, the consortium has experienced many of the positive and negative outcomes of collaborative action. Some of the challenges to be derived from Table 2 become evident in the second-half of the paper where a number of theoretical perspectives are applied to the inter-organisational dynamics and structure of the inland *Waterways* consortium. The paper goes on to conclude with a set of specific recommendations for the consortium as well as offer general directions for future research.

THEORETICAL PERSPECTIVES

The pre-conditions for facilitating collaboration in the case of *Waterways* can be discussed in the context of work conducted by Selin and Chavez (1995)

TABLE 2. Benefits and Drawbacks of Collaboration

Adapted from (Briggs, 1994; Gray, 1989; Jamal & Getz, 1995; Palmer & Bejou, 1995; Selin, 1993; Turner, 1992)

Benefits of Collaboration	Drawbacks of Collaboration
Collaboration offers	*Collaboration can result in:*
• a more effective and efficient means of developing tourism	• fear amongst stakeholders of losing control over the planning and development domain
• an alternative to uneconomic and inefficient 'free market' solutions	• unfamiliarity among stakeholders which can involve the switching of resources to more familiar 'safer' strategies
• a 'vehicle' for the natural congruence of objectives between public/private sector stakeholders	• mutual suspicion and ill-feeling among stakeholders if they are competing with each other for other sources of funds, i.e., EU
• an opportunity for stakeholders to advance shared visions	
• mutual benefit among stakeholders to be derived from the exchange/pooling of resources (time, finance and expertise)	• inertia due to the inherent dynamic tension between competitive and collaborative forces in the tourism system
• the opportunity to spread the cost of new technologies, new innovations and promotional expenditure	• inertia due to the inability of stakeholders to all progress at the same speed
• the reduction/avoidance of unnecessary conflict in the wider tourism system	• general concern over a perceived loss of control over decision-making among stakeholders
• a chance to achieve a greater degree of environmental and sociocultural sustainability	• general scepticism of too many stakeholders being involved to achieve an adequate outcome
• the opportunity for the private sector to allay fears of achieving a desired rate of return from a tourism development	• unhealthy competition with non-collaborating 'honeypot' destinations
• the chance for all stakeholders to reduce risk and uncertainty	• some stakeholders sensing a greater loss of control
• the opportunity to improve the communication of tourism packages to prospective tourists which require complex distribution channels	• ideological/cultural conflict between the public/private sector stakeholders
• more effective representation for some stakeholders	• non-achievement as a consequence of limited time, finance and expertise
• an opportunity for all stakeholders to raise their profile, embark on joint-marketing activities, benefit from joint-research and participate in discussion forums.	

who articulated a five stage process of evolutionary partnership development, notably; antecedents; problem-setting; direction-setting; structuring; and outcomes. This five stage process is the first of a number of theoretical perspectives that will be discussed in relation to the case study.

Antecedents

Networks already established for the promotion of coastal water-based holidays to overseas tourists provided the foundation for the inland *Waterways* consortium, as did the entrepreneurial vision and leadership of key individuals together with the vested interests expressed by a variety of government and trade organisations. Gray (1989) accords great importance to the role and identity of the leadership convenor as a critical component in the early stages of the collaborative initiative. Not only is the convenor responsible for the creation of the initial identity of the venture but they are also responsible for bringing all the interested parties together. In the case study the role of convenor was first played by representatives of the commercial operators Hoseasons and Blakes. However, the real growth in the consortium took place in 1996 with the entrepreneurial influence of the TMS Partnership.

Further background to the partnership formation was the desire to more effectively compete in the international marketplace; the competitive threat from France being particularly strong. The ever decreasing public-purse clearly served as a catalytic focus for local authority interest in the inland *Waterways* consortium which now provides 57 per cent of consortium funding. Coupled with the potential for enhanced economic benefits in terms of overseas visitor spend, the cross-boundary nature of canals and inland waterways provided an additional geographic stimulus for multilateral action in this domain.

Problem-Setting

In view of its membership, the inland *Waterways* consortium generated interest from a number of the key operators in the marketplace. The interdependent nature of the product is clearly reflected by the stakeholders outlined in Table 1. Collective action was deemed beneficial although the non-representation from the small boat-hire operators perhaps signifies their doubt as to who were likely to be the real winners of such an initiative.

Direction-Setting

The direction-setting phase is best illustrated by the agreed aims of the inland *Waterways* consortium. They are:

to increase incremental business to Britain and Ireland by promoting water based holidays in selected generating markets (Germany, Netherlands, Belgium, Norway, Sweden, Denmark, USA, Canada, Australia and New Zealand).

by attracting business to the above niche product, additionally generate income to waterside attractions and facility operators and maximise the tourism potential of an entire area and deliver greater benefits to all parties in the long-run.

The widespread desire to generate additional income along the waterside provides further evidence to explain the healthy representation from local authorities in the inland *Waterways* consortium.

Structuring and Outcomes

The structure of the inland Waterways consortium can best be explained as a programmatic (Waddock, 1989), action-oriented (Witham, 1987) consortium with the programme emphasis being on the implementation of promotional strategies. Consortium members, although pooling funds together, remain essentially independent. If anything, the inland *Waterways* consortium represents a broker for its members whereby it provides overseas marketing assistance. Consortia are particularly popular forms of collaboration with hotels as, like hire-boat operators, they represent the best means for a single hotel to operate effectively in the international marketplace while still retaining a high degree of independence (Byrne, 1993).

The inland *Waterways* consortium is managed by a Steering Group, representation on which is by invitation of the BTA (see Table 1). Quarterly meetings are nominally chaired by the BTA and attendance is normally dominated by the public agencies. Hence, it would appear that the private-sector operators and local authorities are content to pay the relatively modest annual marketing fee without the necessity to become too closely involved except on strategic issues. Membership of the inland *Waterways* consortium is subject to print deadlines three months ahead of the start of the campaign with all funds being collected centrally by the BTA following initial contact by the TMS Partnership. Local authority membership is organised into collectives who contribute to their designated 'region' at a relatively modest fee per region. Private-sector operators and trade organisations pay the same fees as a 'region' of local authorities whilst trade and government agencies pay a slightly higher rate. This is supported with a valuable subsidy from the BTA. In addition, the BTA donates considerable help 'in kind' in the form of press visits, overseas representation and staff support. In terms of outcomes the consortium has three main promotional outlets: a fifty page *Waterways* colour brochure produced in English and German with a total print run of 100,000; a dedicated website managed by the BTA; and an overseas awareness campaign using the overseas offices of the BTA and press visits.

To more accurately define the status of the inland *Waterways* consortium the taxonomy posited by Terpstra and Simonin (1993), and discussed in Palmer and Bejou (1995), provides a suitable framework (see Table 3).

In terms of *coverage*, the inland *Waterways* consortium can be defined as functionally narrow but geographically broad. Its strict promotional remit being offset by pan-British-Irish coverage. In turn, it represents a loosely formed, non-equity alliance *format* whereby although agreeing on specific joint-promotions to their mutual benefit, the financial independence of members is assured. The third characteristic, *mode*, is typified by the intrinsic nature of the relationship among its members. The degree of commitment to the inland *Waterways* consortium from its members is evidenced by a high degree of active participation by the government and trade organisations at the policy stage and the active interest expressed by the local authorities and commercial operators at the strategic decision-making phase. In many instances the convenor provides the key representation for the commercial operators and local authorities. This reflects the confidence of a large number of the consortium members in the ability and direction of the convenor. This is also reflected in the fourth and final characteristic of a consortium alliance,

TABLE 3. A Taxonomy of Co-Marketing Alliance Types

Adapted from Terpstra & Simonin (1993) and Palmer & Bejou (1995)

Distinguishing Characteristics of an Alliance:	Explanatory Note:
COVERAGE	The extensiveness of an alliance with regard to its functional competencies and geographical coverage (Bleeke & Ernst, 1991).
FORM	The constitutional characteristics of an alliance. This can range from a loosely formed non-equity alliance to a formal agreement whereby two or more alliance members purchase an equity stake in other alliance members and increase the dependency of members to each other.
MODE	The intrinsic nature of the relationship among alliance members.
MOTIVE	The underlying reason for the creation of an alliance.

motives. The convenor's sense of vision and championing of the cause are key determinants in the overall ability of the consortium to attract new custom to the inland waterways of Britain and Ireland from overseas. All in all, the inland *Waterways* consortium can be described as an entrepreneurial, opportunity-driven, loosely formed non-equity alliance with a narrow functional but broad geographic focus.

INTER-ORGANISATIONAL DYNAMICS

The six theoretical perspectives posited by Gray and Wood (1991) are used here as a basis to critique the inter-organisational dynamics of the inland *Waterways* consortium (see Table 4). Each of the six theoretical perspectives provide an alternative viewpoint of the inter-organisational domain and provide a valuable framework for the analysis of collaborative organisational forms (Long, 1996).

The *Resource Dependent Theory* represents the first of the six perspectives and is particularly valid in relation to the inland *Waterways* consortium. For the majority of the local authority members of the consortium there is a clear desire to minimise their inter-organisational dependencies and preserve their autonomy and at the same time accept that inter-organisational relationships are necessary to acquire the relevant skills and financial resources to effectively achieve their individual goals. However, although applicable to the local authority members this theory does not adequately explain the rationale behind the two largest commercial operators' membership of the consortium. Compared to the public-sector members, Hoseasons and Blakes Holidays display a considerably higher marketing spend targeted to overseas tourists and demonstrate very active agent based activity in capturing a higher share of the overseas market. Thus, although these parallel promotional strategies are not unique to the commercial operators the extent to which they are both collaborating and competing with each other is. Hence, the attraction for the large commercial operators in maintaining consortium membership is not necessarily financial but driven by the opportunity to develop inter-organisational networks and exert influence on a future potential force in overseas tourism marketing.

The worth of this theoretical perspective is particularly valid in this instance due to the domestic bias of the current demand: 85% of all boat weeks (Edwards et al., 1998). Until the overseas market is fully recognised by all players in the market as important, not just those members of the consortium, then the need to maintain individual autonomy will prevail. The consortium will continue to represent a self-interest driven, and potentially short-term, collaborative initiative rather than one which is to seriously chal-

TABLE 4. Theoretical Perspectives of Inter-Organisational Collaboration

Adapted from Gray & Wood (1991)

Theoretical Perspective:	Explanatory Note:
RESOURCE DEPENDENT	The focus of this theory rests on the minimisation of inter-organisational dependency and the preservation of the organisation's autonomy, while at the same time recognising that inter-organisational relationships are necessary for the acquisition of resources. The theory advances a number of 'domain' questions such as the circumstances in which stakeholders adopt collaborative alliances and the patterns of interdependencies that result from resource exchanges.
CORPORATE SOCIAL PERFORMANCE	This theoretical perspective addresses the degree to which alliance members are able to achieve corporate benefits through the fulfillment of social and wider environmental objectives via collaborative action.
STRATEGIC MANAGEMENT	The means by which organisations are able to minimise external threats and maximise external opportunities by means of collaborating with others. One of the key 'domain' level questions to be raised is the extent to which collaborative action regulates the self-serving behaviour of the alliance members so that collective gains are achieved.
MICROECONOMICS	This theory focuses on the efficiency of a collaborative alliance as an inter-organisational form and questions the impediments to inter-organisational transactional efficiency.
INSTITUTIONAL THEORY/ NEGOTIATED ORDER	The means by which inter-organisational entities interact and are shaped by institutional environments, ideologies and norms. Negotiated Order Theory focuses on the symbolic and perceptual aspects of inter-organisational relationships. In particular, it elucidates the evolution of shared understandings among alliance members of the domain's structures, processes, limits and possibilities.
POLITICAL	This theory addresses the power dynamics and the distribution of benefits within a network of collaborating partners in a problem domain.

lenge the 'problem domain' of collectively attracting more overseas tourists to the inland waterways of Britain and Ireland.

The second theory posited by Gray and Wood (1991), that of *Corporate Social Performance*, does not clearly coincide with the collective goals of the inland *Waterways* consortium. This is not, however, a weakness on the part of the theory, more a missed opportunity for the consortium. With its overriding emphasis on promotion, the inland *Waterways* consortium does not as yet demonstrate any evidence as to its capacity to perform the roles of an active social institution. For example, in view of the importance attributed to sustainable tourism over the past decade (Garrod & Fyall, 1998), the extent to which the consortium has mediated between the interests of its members and those of the wider environment is open to debate. Although accepting the principles of sustainable tourism the inland *Waterways* consortium has at its disposal the ability to more actively develop a clear mandate for sustainable tourism development. Hence, its span of influence could spread out beyond mere promotion to a number of actions including:

- sustainable product development
- waterside community regeneration
- cross-boundary product interpretation

The ability of the consortium to represent some form of collaborative social institution in the future could prove to be a crucial ingredient in the sourcing of external funds, be they domestic, EU or from a private sponsor/lender. This in turn could enhance the overall quality of the experience for tourists and improve the quality of life for the waterside host communities; the social institutional context then representing a more explicit dimension of the inland *Waterways* consortium rather than the incumbent, relatively product-inactive, dimension.

As with the theory of corporate social performance the third theoretical perspective posited by Gray and Wood (1991), the *Strategic Management Theory*, contributes little to the overall understanding of the inter-organisational dynamics of the inland *Waterways* consortium. However, *Microeconomic Theory*, which examines the overall efficiency of resource use within an entire inter-organisational network, does offer some useful insights (Long, 1996). On the one hand there appears to be significant efficiency gains to be derived from collaboration on the part of the local authorities. Joint-promotion activity through the consortium enables local authorities to have a presence in the international marketplace which otherwise would be beyond their reach. On the other hand, some of the private-sector operators may consider the duplication of overseas promotional effort and overall degree of synergy to be derived from membership of the consortium of limited benefit; although this issue is only of relevance if one considers the economic cost in isolation.

Where *Microeconomic Theory* does lend weight to a greater understanding of the inland *Waterways* consortium is in its contribution to 'free rider' effects. In this instance, 'free rider' effects relate to benefits derived by collaborating partners incommensurate with their contribution to the inter-organisational alliance. Gray and Wood (1991) question the extent to which organisational collectives can overcome 'free rider' effects and other impediments to enhance the efficiency of their transactions. This is particularly appropriate *vis-à-vis* some of the trade and government organisation members of the consortium who, although displaying disproportionate power in the Steering Group, contribute limited sums in terms of financial resources. The overall benefit to the local authorities and commercial operators of such collaborative partners would be put to the test if the consortium was to adopt a more dynamic, broader product development remit.

Of more constructive benefit to the understanding of the inland *Waterways* consortium is the contribution of *Institutional/Negotiated Order Theory*. 'The central premise of institutional theory is that organisations seek to achieve legitimacy from institutional actors by structurally adjusting to institutional influences' (Gray & Wood, 1991). This theoretical perspective applies well to the inland *Waterways* consortium as it highlights the evolution of the consortium from the originating coastal *Waterfront* initiative and the earlier catalyst, the 'Great British Cities' group. The institutional norms of the coastal *Waterfront* consortium clearly represented familiar territory for many inland *Waterways* members as well as providing a sound promotional platform for prospective new membership. In terms of achieving legitimacy among its members, representation from all sectors (governmental, private and trade) coupled with the tangible 'promotional' output collectively address the issue. Moreover, one can postulate that the whole issue of collaboration is a characteristic of contemporary government and is reinforced by their funding agencies. The inland *Waterways* consortium neatly dovetails with the BTA's adoption of market segmentation strategies and is testament to the BTA acting as enabler rather than provider in the longer-term. It also clearly mirrors those five criteria identified by Long (1997) earlier in the paper. Above all the creation of the inland *Waterways* consortium reflects:

- the erosion of local government powers and resources and the increased recognition from local government of the necessity and value of partnerships with other agencies,
- the catalytic role of the national tourist boards in the formulation of partnership arrangements and the more recent reduction in their resources for this purpose.

In tandem with the above, the *Negotiated Order Theory* raises the question of the symbolic and perceptual aspects of inter-organisational relationships;

particularly on the evolution of shared understandings among stakeholders of the domain's structures and processes, limits and possibilities. Although the inland *Waterways* consortium has a clear 'promotional' remit one suspects that some members view the consortium as a symbolic 'quick fix' solution to the attraction of more overseas visitors to their areas with the existence of colour promotional material and overseas presence providing tangible evidence of the consortium's achievements. Further research is required to investigate this aspect as an overly high symbolic content, as perceived by the consortium members, would limit the overall effectiveness of both competitive and collaborative marketing activity in attracting overseas tourists to the inland waterways of Britain and Ireland.

The final theory put forward by Gray and Wood (1991) as a means to facilitate understanding of inter-organisational behaviour is that of *Political Theory*. This theory, which has its origins in private interests and conflict, elucidates the issues of power and influence over resources within collaborative initiatives and is of direct relevance to the inter-organisational dynamics of the inland *Waterways* consortium. The theory demonstrates particular resonance with regard to the over representation of trade and government organisations on the Steering Group of the inland *Waterways* consortium. It provides the foundations for the understanding of possible conflict between the public mindset of the trade, government and local authority members and the private-entrepreneurial mindset of the commercial operators and lead convenor.

More recent work by Palmer (1998) addresses the issue of intra-collaborative compatibility and questions those factors which contribute to long-term mutually beneficial relationships. His viewpoint that collaborative partners do not necessarily have to like each other to gain benefit from inter-organisational activity reasserts the relevance of the resource dependent theory proposed by Gray and Wood (1991). It also emphasises the fact that inter-organisational links are often established to create 'negotiated environments' to deal with problems of uncertainty and dependence (Palmer, 1998:189). Previous relationships between collaborative parties often impact on behaviour within the new collaborative entity.

Since its launch in 1996 the inland Waterways consortium has relied on a great deal of goodwill and trust in furthering its overall degree of collaborative effectiveness. Its loose style of governance, although integral to the early stages of consortium development, is typified by unrepresentative 'Steering Group' decision making which is frequently slow and often an impediment to creative pro-active policy formulation. As with many collaborative initiatives, too loose a structure can also result in some members becoming encapsulated in endless meetings whilst other members, often in the private sector, end up conducting unilateral action, often to the detriment of the collaborative initiative. Although there is no clear evidence of this yet happening in the inland *Waterways* consortium the time may arrive whereby the benefits of a much tighter style of collaborative governance and a corresponding change in its inter-organisational structure are too rewarding to reject. These would be decisive leadership, sufficient administrative support, a tight focus, and transparent implementation of policies; all augured by Palmer (1998) as essential governance criteria for a sustainable collaborative entity.

CONCLUSION

In 1995, work conducted by Selin and Chavez identified the need to expand the current paucity of case research on tourism collaborative activity. This paper has examined one specific collaborative entity, the inland *Waterways* consortium, in an attempt to advance existing knowledge of the internal dynamics of an inter-organisational collaborative tourism initiative. With reference to the six theoretical perspectives on inter-organisational collaboration posited by Gray and Wood (1991) this paper has critically appraised these perspectives and discussed their relevance to the inland *Waterways* consortium. Further work by Gray (1985, 1989); Jamal & Getz (1995); Long (1997); Palmer (1998); Palmer & Bejou (1995) and Wood & Gray (1991) has provided much of the additional theoretical underpinning.

The fact that such a wide range of public and private sector organisations shoulder responsibilities for delivering the tangible and intangible components of the inland waterways boating holiday product serves as the catalytic focus for the origins of collaborative activity on the inland waterways of Britain and Ireland. The genesis of the consortium is largely explained by the structural adjustment of the sector and national tourist authority (BTA) to institutional influences or *Institutional Order Theory* (Gray & Wood, 1991). The previous experience of many members of the consortium in earlier partnership schemes such as 'Great British cities' and Waterfront initiatives represented familiar territory for many members and provided tangible evidence of the work and value of such partnerships. The timing is also particularly relevant to the continued reduction in public spending and the attempt to introduce greater marketing efficiency at the BTA, with limited resources, by adopting market segmentation strategies. It would appear that this institutional context is not fully developed by Selin and Chavez's (1995) five stage evolutionary partnership development model and it is proposed that it could be incorporated more explicitly into the 'antecedents' stage of their model.

However, the main contribution of the Selin and Chavez (1995) model to understanding the formation and dynamics of the *Waterways* consortium is the emphasis attached to the role and identity of the convenor. This role is further reinforced if one considers, in the context of Terpstra and Simonin's

(1993) taxonomy, the motives of the convenor as being entrepreneurial, opportunity-driven with a narrow functional but broad geographic focus. Although there is broad public sector support for the consortium it is proposed that the entrepreneurial nature of the convenor has contributed to the growth of the partnership.

Now in only its third year of operation it would appear that the inland *Waterways* consortium is reaching a crucial stage in its evolution. The inter-organisational dynamics, most notably its loose style of governance with slow, public sector dominated decision-making, appear to frequently be an impediment to pro-active policy formulation. A future change to a tighter style of collaborative governance proposed by Palmer (1998) may be an option for the future.

In view of the above, the most important outcome of this paper is the fact that collaboration is to be regarded as an emergent, dynamic process, a process which requires far greater research before one is able to postulate a uniform 'collaboration life cycle.' In many ways the principal purpose of this paper has been to stimulate discussion among members of marketing consortia similar to *Waterways* as to the future mission, format and desired output of their collaborative entities. In view of the findings of this paper a number of propositions are offered to members of the inland *Waterways* consortium to stimulate debate and to serve as a catalyst to expand upon their inter-organisational collaborative marketing initiative.

RECOMMENDATIONS

The specific recommendations derived from this study can be split into three categories. Recommendations which relate to the 'sense of purpose' of the consortium are included under *Mission*, those which refer to the structure of the consortium under *Format* and, finally, those which detail potential outcomes are chronicled under *Desired Output*. It is the intention of the authors to review the implementation of some/all of these recommendations as the consortium progresses into its third year of operation and examine the extent to which they contribute to the overall effectiveness of this inter-organisational collaborative marketing alliance.

Mission

- Enhance membership understanding of the interdependent nature of the inland waterway boating holiday product and the problem domain, and corresponding need for collaboration.
- Clearly demonstrate to members the achievements and future direction of collaboration providing timescales and measured outcomes where possible.

- Promote the idea of a domain champion; a lead convenor who can propagate a domain mentality, facilitate future collaborative activity and initiate interest among non-participants, in particular small commercial operators, the visitor attractions sector and special event co-ordinators.
- Demonstrate the need to move beyond a self-interest and promotional remit to a more domain focused form of collaboration. This could seek to actively develop the inland waterways boating holiday product via branding, interpretation schemes and integrated booking systems.
- Advance the strategic focus of collaboration and the need for longer-term participative and financial commitment from collaborating partners.

Format

- Develop an inter-organisational culture which is domain driven.
- Develop internal processes and structures which maximise inter-organisational synergy and limit the opportunity for self-interest driven policies.
- Create a collaborative structure which facilitates the sourcing of external funds.
- Stress the benefits to be derived from a more commercially-driven, tighter collaborative governance style in the face of ever increasing and more widespread competition from overseas markets.
- Maintain the endorsement of national tourist and trade related organisations to enhance overall collaboration credibility.
- Develop a structure which accommodates the views of the local waterside host communities since interaction with the local community is an important determinant of product satisfaction for overseas tourists to Britain and Ireland's inland waterways (Edwards et al., 1998).

Desired Output

- Provide a coherent package of marketing assistance to collaborating partners in the form of promotional and product development, visitor management initiatives, integrated booking systems, market research and marketing information systems.
- Enhance inter-organisational communication via promotions and special event formats.

All in all, this paper demonstrates the inter-organisational dynamics of a contemporary entity through theoretical perspectives. The relative youth of the inland *Waterways* consortium prohibits an overly critical analysis but serves as the stimulus for more intense investigation in the future as it seeks to raise the volume of overseas visitors to the inland waterways of Britain and Ireland. Hence, a number of further areas of research warrant future attention. In particular, the seminal work by Gray and Wood (1991) and Selin and Chavez (1995) can again be used to facilitate interpretation of the evolutionary dynamics of the inland *Waterways* consortium; a longitudinal study over a 3 year timescale which incorporates all collaborative partners perhaps representing the most useful means of advancing our understanding of an increasingly common type of initiative.

REFERENCES

Anderson, J., & Narus, J. (1990). A model of distributor firm and manufacturer firm working partnerships. *Journal of Marketing*, 54: 42-58.

Bleeke, J., & Ernst, D. (1991). The way to win in cross-border alliances. *Harvard Business Review*, 67 (6): 127-135.

Boivin, C. (1987). Public-private sector interactions in Canada. In *Travel and Tourism: Thrive or Survive*, conference proceedings, pp. 147-150. Salt Lake City: Travel and Tourism Research Association.

Briggs, S. (1994). Powerful Partnerships: Setting Up and Running a Marketing Consortium. London: English Tourist Board Insights (A69-A72).

Brown, L.D. (1980). Planned change in underorganised systems. In Cummings, T.G. (ed), *Systems Theory for Organisation Development*. New York: John Wiley & Sons.

Byrne, A. (1993). International hotel consortia. In Jones, P., & Pizam, A. (eds), *The International Hospitality Industry-Organisational and Operational Issues*. New York: John Wiley & Sons.

Crompton, J. (1990). Claiming our share of the tourism dollar. *Parks and Recreation*, 8 (2): 42-47.

Edwards, C., Fyall, A., Oakley, B., & Weiss, A. (1998). Boating holidays: Opportunities in Britain. *English Tourist Board Insights*, (B67-B81), London.

Garrod, B., & Fyall, A. (1998). Beyond the rhetoric of sustainable tourism? *Tourism Management*, 19 (3): 199-212.

Gill, A., & Williams, P. (1994). Managing growth in mountain tourism communities. *Tourism Management*, 15 (3): 212-220.

Gray, B. (1985). Conditions facilitating interorganizational collaboration. *Human Relations*, 38: 911-936.

Gray, B. (1989). *Collaborating: Finding Common Ground for Multiparty Problems*. San Francisco: Jossey-Bass.

Gray, B., & Wood, D.J. (1991). Collaborative alliances: Moving from theory to practice. *Journal of Applied Behavioural Science*, 27 (1): 3-22.

Gunn, C. (1994). *Tourism Planning: Basics, Concepts, Cases* (3rd ed.). Washington, DC: Taylor & Francis.

Holder, J. (1992). The need for public-private sector co-operation in tourism. *Tourism Management*, 13 (2): 157-162.

Hoseason, J. (1990). Boating holidays: Opportunities in Britain. *English Tourist Board Insights*, (B8.1-B8.11), London.

Inskeep, E. (1991). *Tourism Planning: An Integrated and Sustainable Development Approach*. New York: Van Nostrand Reinhold.

Jamal, T.B., & Getz, D. (1995). Collaboration theory and community tourism planning. *Annals of Tourism Research*, 22 (1): 186-204.

Levine, S., & White, P.E. (1961). Exchange as a conceptual framework for the study of interorganizational relations. *Administrative Science Quarterly*, 5: 583-601.

Long, P. (1996). Inter-organisational collaboration in the development of tourism and the arts 1996: Year of visual arts. In Robinson, M. et al. (eds), *Culture as the Tourist Product*, pp. 235-252. Sunderland: Business Education Publishers Ltd.

Long, P. (1997). Researching tourism partnership organisations: From practice to theory to methodology. In Murphy, P.E. (ed), *Quality Management in Urban Tourism*, pp. 235-252. Chichester: John Wiley & Sons.

Macneil, I. (1974). The many futures of contract. *Southern Californian Law Review*, 57: 691-816.

Macneil, I. (1980). *The New Social Contract: An Inquiry into Modern Contractual Relations*. New Haven: Yale University Press.

McGinnis, D. (1992). The changing image of Jackson Hole, Wyoming. *In Mountain Resort Development*, Proceedings of the Vail Conference, pp. 126-136. Burnaby: The Simon Fraser University Center for Tourism Policy and Research.

Murphy, P. (1985). *Tourism: A Community Affair*. New York: Methuen.

Oaks, S. (1992). Design and community development in the mountain resort community of Vail, Colorado: A comparative look at effects of the Town of Vail Master Plan Hazard Reduction Strategies 1974-1991. In *Mountain Resort Development*, Proceedings of the Vail Conference, p. 55. Burnaby: The Simon Fraser University Center for Tourism Policy and Research.

Oppenheim, A.N. (1992). *Questionnaire Design, Interviewing and Attitude Measurement*. London: Pinter.

Osborne, D., & Gaebler, T. (1992). *Reinventing Government*. Reading, MA: Addison-Wesley.

Page, S. (1995). *Urban Tourism*. London: Routledge.

Palmer, A., & Bejou, D. (1995). Tourism destination marketing alliances. *Annals of Tourism Research*, 22 (3): 616-629.

Palmer, A. (1996). Linking external and internal relationship building in networks of public and private sector organisations: a case study. *International Journal of Public Sector Management*, 9 (3): 51-60.

Palmer, A. (1998). Evaluating the governance style of marketing groups. *Annals of Tourism Research*, 25 (1): 185-201.

Pearce, D. (1992). *Tourist Organisations*. Harlow: Longman.

Pfeffer, J., & Salanick, G. (1978). *The External Control of Organisation: A Resource Dependence Perspective*. New York: Harper and Row.

Reve, T. (1992). Horizontal and vertical alliances in industrial marketing channels. In Frazier, G. (ed), *Advances in Distribution Channel Research*, pp. 235-257. Greenwich: JAI Press.

Ritchie, J.R.B. (1993). Crafting a destination vision: Putting the concept of resident responsive tourism into practice. *Tourism Management*, 14 (5): 279-389.

Schmidt, S.M., & Kochan, T.A. (1977). Interorganizational relationships: Patterns and motivations. *Administrative Science Quarterly*, 22: 220-234.

Selin, S. (1993). Collaborative alliances: New interorganizational forms in tourism. *Journal of Travel & Tourism Marketing*, 2 (2/3): 217-227.

Selin, S., & Chavez, D. (1995). Developing an evolutionary tourism partnership model. *Annals of Tourism Research*, 22 (4): 844-856.

Smith, B. (1991). New horizons in tourism and hospitality education, training and research. *Journal of Travel Research*, 30 (2): 51-52.

Stern, L., & Reve, T. (1990). Distribution channels as political economies. *Journal of Marketing*, 44 (3): 52-64.

Stevens, B. (1988). Co-operative activities in competitive markets. In *Tourism Research: Exploring Boundaries*, pp. 139-141. Salt Lake City: Travel and Tourism Research Association.

Terpstra, V., & Simonin, B. (1993). Strategic alliances in the triad. *Journal of International Marketing*, 1: 4-25.

Trist, E.L. (1977). Collaboration in work settings: A personal perspective. *The Journal of Applied Behavioural Sciences*, 13: 268-278.

Turner, G. (1992). Public/private sector partnership-panacea or passing phase? *English Tourist Board Insights*, (A85-A91), London.

Waddock, S. (1989). Understanding social partnerships. *Administration and Society*, 21 (2): 78-100.

Williamson, O. (1975). *Markets and Hierarchies*. New York: The Free Press.

Withiam, G. (1987). Unchained melody: How independent hotels work in harmony. *Cornell H.R.A. Quarterly*, 28 (2): 77-80.

Witt, S.F., & Moutinho, L. (1989). *Tourism Marketing and Management Handbook*. New York: Prentice Hall.

Wood, D.J., & Gray, B. (1991). Toward a comprehensive theory of collaboration. *Journal of Applied Behavioural Science*, 27 (2): 139-162.

Relationships
in the Distribution Channel of Tourism:
Conflicts Between Hoteliers
and Tour Operators
in the Mediterranean Region

Dimitrios Buhalis

SUMMARY. This paper examines industrial relationships in the distribution channel of tourism. Distribution becomes one of the most significant elements of tourism marketing as it determines all other aspects of the marketing mix. This paper concentrates on the conflict experienced in the distribution channel between hoteliers and tour operators in the Mediterranean summer/seaside resort context. It attempts to illuminate the area, to identify significant variables for its assessment and to provide a solid background for further research on the topic. Research in Greece demonstrates that Mediterranean hoteliers increasingly find the power of tour operators from Northern European countries very challenging. Similarly with other intermediaries, in order for tour operators to remain competitive in the marketplace they reduce the profit margins of their suppliers at destinations and thus reduce the profitability levels of enterprises and the economic impacts at destinations. *[Article copies available for a fee from The Haworth Document Delivery Service: 1-800-342-9678. E-mail address: getinfo@haworthpressinc.com <Website: http://www.haworthpressinc.com>]*

Dimitrios Buhalis is Senior Lecturer in Tourism, University of Westminster, 35 Marylebone Road, London, NW1 5LS, England (e-mail: buhalid@wmin.ac.uk).

[Haworth co-indexing entry note]: "Relationships in the Distribution Channel of Tourism: Conflicts Between Hoteliers and Tour Operators in the Mediterranean Region." Buhalis, Dimitrios. Co-published simultaneously in *International Journal of Hospitality & Tourism Administration* (The Haworth Press, Inc.) Vol. 1, No. 1, 2000, pp. 113-139; and: *Global Alliances in Tourism and Hospitality Management* (ed: John C. Crotts, Dimitrios Buhalis, and Roger March) The Haworth Press, Inc., 2000, pp. 113-139. Single or multiple copies of this article are available for a fee from The Haworth Document Delivery Service [1-800-342-9678, 9:00 a.m. - 5:00 p.m. (EST). E-mail address: getinfo@haworthpressinc.com].

113

KEYWORDS. Strategic alliances, business relationships

1. DISTRIBUTION CHANNELS IN THE TOURISM INDUSTRY

Distribution channels are increasingly regarded as one of the most critical elements in marketing, as they determine the competitiveness and profitability of organisations (Christopher, 1991; Gattorna, 1990; Stern and El-Ansary, 1992). Tourism distribution channels attract more attention by contemporary researchers and strategists. Their purpose is twofold: to provide *information* for prospective tourists and intermediaries as well as to establish a mechanism which would enable consumers to make, confirm and pay for *reservations* (Middleton, 1994; Bitner and Booms, 1982; Welburn, 1987; Holloway, 1998). "In tourism, the position of the distribution sector is much stronger: trade intermediaries (travel agents and tour operators of course, but also charter brokers, reservation systems and other travel distribution specialists) have a far greater power to influence and to direct demand than their counterparts in other industries do. Since they do, in fact, control demand, they also have increased bargaining power in their relations with suppliers of tourist services and are in a position to influence their pricing, their product policies and their promotional activities" (WTO, 1975).

Several scholars attempt to define the tourism distribution channel concept. Middleton (1994) proposes that "a distribution channel is any organised and serviced system, created or utilised to provide convenient points of sale and/or access to consumers, away from the location of production and consumption, and paid for out of marketing budgets." However, this definition ignores the promotional and marketing research activities undertaken by the channels, while it underestimates their information provision function. It also excludes local outlets, such as box offices or incoming travel agencies at destinations. Furthermore, McIntosh defines tourism distribution channels, as "an operating structure, system or linkages of various combinations of travel organisation, through which a producer of travel products describes and confirms travel arrangements to the buyer" (Mill and Morrison, 1985). The promotional element is still ignored but, the information provision function is highlighted. Moreover, the World Tourism Organisation (WTO, 1975) suggests that "a distribution channel can be described as a given combination of intermediaries who co-operate in the sale of a product. It follows that a distribution system can be and in most instances is composed of more than one distribution channel, each of which operates parallel to and in competition with other channels." Perhaps more accurately Wanhill (1998) suggests that "the principal role of intermediaries is to bring buyers and sellers together, either to create markets where they previously did not exist or to make existing markets work more efficiently and thereby to expand market size."

Several generic functions and benefits are therefore enhanced by the tourism distribution channel, as illustrated in Figure 1.

Consumers may purchase various components directly from producers, while numerous distribution and sales intermediaries are involved in promoting and distributing the tourism product. There are endless variations of the tourism distribution channel, depending on each particular industry structure and external environment. Often ad hoc partnerships are established be-

FIGURE 1. Functions of the tourism distribution channel

☐ Identify consumers' needs, requests and expected experiences

☐ Assemble tourism products from different providers according to customer expectations

☐ Provision of co-ordinated and seamless tourism products

☐ Facilitate the selling process by reserving and issuing travel documents

☐ Reduction of prices by negotiating and pre-purchasing tourism products in bulk

☐ Ameliorate inventory management by managing demand and supply

☐ Issue and deliver travel documentation, i.e., ticketing, vouchers, etc.

☐ Assessment of quality of facilities and products

☐ Assistance in legal requirements for consumers (e.g., visas) and suppliers

☐ Facilitate communications between consumers and suppliers especially in multilingual and multicultural environments

☐ Reduce the perceived risk for consumers

☐ Provision of information by using leaflets, maps, brochures, video, CDs

☐ Consumers guidance/advice/consultation

☐ Undertake pre- and post- experience marketing research

☐ Facilitation of access to often remote tourism products, for both bookings and purchasing

☐ Establish a clearing system where each channel member receives payments for their services

☐ Spreading the commercial risk involved between channel members

☐ Arranging details and ancillary services, such as insurance, visa, currency, etc.

☐ Assume risk when pre-purchasing tourism products

☐ Promotion of particular products or packages, in co-operation with suppliers

☐ Promotion of distressed capacity in low period and at the last minute

☐ Complaint handling for both customers and industry

tween channel members to satisfy specific demand or to provide services requested by consumers. The literature often refers to two different types of intermediaries, i.e., tour operators (wholesalers) and outgoing travel agencies (retailers) (Gee, Makens, Choy, 1989; Holloway, 1998; Beaver, 1993; Renshaw, 1997; Laws, 1997). Leisure tourism distribution channels normally include some more members. For example, incoming/handling travel agencies based at destinations undertake the handling of incoming groups. Moreover, national or regional tourist organisations and Destination Management Organisations are used by both tourists and travel trade for additional information, support documentation, classification and inspection of tourism products, co-operation in promotion, and special arrangements. Furthermore, a number of organisations offer ancillary services and may also be considered as tourism distribution channel members. These include speciality intermediaries, clubs, credit card companies, special privileged user cards, societies, religious groups and organisations (Wanhill, 1998; Mill and Morrison, 1985; Gee, Makens, Choy, 1989; Middleton, 1994).

Middleton (1994) highlights that "paradoxically, the inability in travel and tourism to create physical stocks of products, adds to rather than reduces the importance of the distribution process. In marketing practice, creating and manipulating access for consumers is one of the principal ways to *manage demand* for highly perishable products." Contemporary channels not only distribute tourism products, but also influence all the other elements of the marketing mix. For example, channels often determine the price by assessing real-time demand and available supply; manipulate and formulate tourism products by combining and tailoring products according to customers' needs and wishes; and finally facilitate promotion by targeting specific markets and establishing communication. Hence, tourism distribution decisions are critical for tourism enterprises, as they influence their entire marketing mix. Suitable intermediaries should be utilised by suppliers, as they influence both branding and image of tourism products. Tourism distribution channels vary according to products, industry structures and countries. Although similar principles normally apply there are several significant differences which prevent generalisations. This paper concentrates on the European leisure market and in particular on the summer Mediterranean seaside resorts.

2. CONFLICTS WITHIN THE TOURISM DISTRIBUTION CHANNEL: HOTELS vs. TOUR OPERATORS

Since each member of the tourism distribution channel has different commercial and strategic interests, as well as operational procedures, several intra-channel conflicts emerge inevitably. A major source of conflict is usually the incompatibility and antagonism between targets and goals set by each partner.

As each channel member attempts to protect and advance its own interests, they tend to exert a variety of power forces on their partners in order to achieve their objectives, often at the expense of their partners' gains. A variety of conflicts are evident in tourism distribution channels. These conflicts emerge from four major sources. Firstly, the *price and profit margin distribution* generate inter-channel conflict. Consumers have a certain budget for their holidays and therefore channel members compete directly with their partners for a larger share. Secondly, the exceeding *vertical integration generates oligopolistic behaviour*, which reduces the negotiation power of small/ independent channel partners and jeopardises their competitiveness. Thirdly, several *operational issues* can also generate conflicts often as partners fail to fulfil their obligations and/or provide the service they promised. Fourthly, as bankruptcies, mergers and take-overs are not unusual in the tourism distribution channel, partners' *financial security* is often quoted as a major source of conflict. The limited financial commitments and assets required by travel intermediaries make this industry extremely volatile. The following analysis examines the major conflicts between hotels and tour operators, from the former's point of view. The analysis also illuminates the sources of conflict and examines which types of hotels face this problem more than others and why.

Conflicts between hotels and tour operators are frequent in the tourism industry. They can be both operational and strategic. At the strategic level, the objectives of hotels and tour operators are antagonistic and incompatible to a certain extent as the two partners compete within the channel in order to maximise their financial benefit. Tour operators and in particular the larger/ mass ones attempt to increase their profitability by enlarging their market share and volume, through offering inexpensively priced holiday packages. In contrast, hotels have to balance the volume of clients they serve with their average room rates, in order to maximise their yield and achieve a reasonable return on investment. Volume of business is not necessarily the best strategy, as it may jeopardise their image, profit margins and long term profitability.

The proliferation of tourism supply in many destinations world-wide, combined with a lower growth of demand, enables both consumers and the travel trade to increase their bargaining power over suppliers. Almost unlimited and undifferentiated supply in numerous destinations around the world essentially increasingly forces the industry to compete on a "cost advantage" basis. The vast majority of suppliers are Small and Medium-sized Tourism Enterprises (SMTEs). Due to the structural and functional weaknesses of most SMTEs, hotels depend almost entirely on tour operators for their communications with consumers and visibility in their major markets (Buhalis, 1994). In addition, through vertical integration, tour operators control both transportation companies (charter airlines) and retailers (travel agency chains). Therefore such firms have established their position as channel leaders of the distribution channel (Josephides, 1993 and 1994; Renshaw, 1994; Monopolies and Merger Commission, 1986, 1989 and 1997; Baywater, 1992, 1994 and 1997; O'Brien, 1996; Howitt, 1995). Moreover, exclusivity rights (i.e., the right of tour operators to exclusively represent hotels in their markets), provide tour operators with control over hotels' distribution mix, as they effectively determine which other channel member can feature a particular establishment in their programme. These conflicts are evident not only on the Mediterranean industry but also on several destinations around the world (Sinclair et al., 1992; Bote and Sinclair, 1991; Shaw and Williams, 1994; Valenzuela, 1991; Britton, 1989; Sheldon, 1994; Roekaerts and Savat, 1989; Ottaway, 1992; Allen, 1985). These conflicts generate an enormous pressure on principals to reduce their prices. They also reduce the economic impacts of tourism at the macro level. As a result, a consumption of local resources can be observed in most destinations, while very few initiatives are undertaken to sustain the invaluable environmental and cultural wealth of these regions.

A great differentiation between small/independent and large/mass tour operators can be observed, due to their dissimilar strategies. Most conflicts between hotels and tour operators are generated by large/mass operators, rather than small/niche ones. Small/niche operators, as for example the members of the Association of Independent Tour Operators (AITO) in the UK tend to have a greater commitment to properties and destinations. Hence, they are often considered by hoteliers as partners and even friends. They tend to concentrate more on quality and normally have higher quality standards and very loyal customers. Some of their products are specialised and often have specific requirements, which they are prepared to pay for. However, hoteliers appreciated that smaller tour operators have to compete in their marketplace with larger counterparts and thus they also require competitive and comparable pricing. In addition, tour operators from different countries have different attitudes and priorities. Typically, larger British, Scandinavian and Dutch operators are concerned with price, whilst German, American and Japanese operators seek value for money and hence are prepared to pay for better quality. This often reflects the level of competition in their home markets, as well as the orientation, values, needs and wants of their clientele.

Leisure/summer hotels in the Mediterranean region seem to have chronic and unbearable conflicts with tour operators, which they feel unable to resolve. This is partly because of their marketing and management weaknesses; incompetence and insecurity to find new partners; the fact that they get accustomed to the situation and become idle; and also to the dominance of tour operators in the industry. An in-depth analysis of these conflicts as perceived by Greek hoteliers is conducted in the following paragraphs.

3. RESEARCH METHODOLOGY

The bulk of the research analysed here took place on the Aegean Islands in Greece in 1993. In addition, a second, smaller scale, follow up qualitative survey was conducted in 1996 and 1998. This research used *in-depth, structured personal interviews* in order to collect sufficient data to support both the descriptive and exploratory research. Personal interviews were regarded as the only data-collection method which could provide the response rate and the wealth of information required in order to support both qualitative and quantitative analysis. Personal interviews also established an element of trust between hoteliers and the researcher and enable them to offer truthful and accurate answers. However, as the Aegean region is spread over a 95 inhabited islands archipelago, most of which have some types of tourism amenities, it was impossible to visit all of them for the field research. Hence an additional mail survey was undertaken for hotels on remote islands in order to increase the number of respondents as well as to verify that similar problems and issues are relevant to all areas on the Aegean islands.

Previous research and professional experience had demonstrated that hoteliers had identified their distribution channel as a major handicap for their operations and profitability. As a result the researcher developed a brief which was then discussed with key hoteliers and executives from the Greek National Tourism Organisation and the National and Regional Hotel Associations, as well as other researchers/academics. Unstructured interviews with 18 senior professionals enabled the identification of problems and the establishment of suitable variables for their measurement. They also illuminated this under-researched area and provided the background knowledge for developing and undertaking the survey. Following this phase a detailed semi-structured questionnaire was developed and was sent for comment and feedback to several interviewees.

The entire population of 1691 hotels on the Aegean Islands were targeted for the survey. A pilot study of personal interviews was undertaken on the islands of Kos and Chios. After adjusting the research instruments a full scale survey was undertaken on the islands of Kos, Rhodos, Lesvos and Limnos. All hotels on all other Aegean Islands were targeted through the mail survey. It is estimated that about 500 accommodation establishments were visited, and 241 interviews were completed (18 in the pilot study and 223 during the field research). The overall response rate to the in-depth interview attempts was 48.2%. The rest of the owners/managers were either unavailable during the period of the research, extremely busy or unwilling to offer an interview. Encouragingly however, the vast majority were supportive and thought that more research should be undertaken on the topic, while most properties which denied an interview often had reasons beyond their owner/managers' control. Out of 1000 questionnaires posted a further 63 responses were received from accommodation establishments through the mail survey. Hence the total of completed questionnaires used was 304. This represents about 18% of the Aegean total accommodation units, resulting in a coverage of 46.8% of the total capacity in beds. Hence proprietors/managers of almost half the Aegean supply participated in this research. The geographical distribution of the sample spread over 23 islands.

In-depth unstructured discussions with tourism industry entrepreneurs, executives and researchers/academics, as well as with Information Technology (IT) experts and GNTO executives were used throughout the research process. They contributed significantly to the understanding and conceptualisation of the major problems and challenges, the design of the research methodology and instruments as well as with the interpretation of the results. Qualitative research was instrumental in the research process and analysis. The following analysis offers a blend between qualitative and quantitative techniques. Descriptive statistics are employed in order to explore the nature and strength of each problem. In addition, X^2 tests and R correlations are undertaken in order to explain the reasons for the emerging conflicts, as well as the variables which seem to determine the seriousness of the problem. Although many R correlations presented here are weak, it is important to highlight their statistical significance in order to explore the issues in further research and illustrate which sub-variables hold stronger interrelations.

The *second wave qualitative survey* in 1996 and in 1998 was undertaken with key entrepreneurs as well as with the Directors of Hoteliers Associations and Tourism Boards. The purpose of this survey was to establish if any changes were experienced during the research period as well as to elaborate and clarify research findings emerging from the quantitative research. As there is no literature and research on this area, the purpose of the research was twofold: to illuminate the area by providing a better understanding of motives, realities and conflicts and also to establish variables for further research on the area.

4. CONFLICTS BETWEEN MEDITERRANEAN HOTELS AND TOUR OPERATORS

A wide range of conflicts were reported by hotels in their relationships with tour operators, although when asked directly whether they have any problems with tour operators, only 37.3% responded positively. Evidently, hotels which depend for the majority of their customers on their first and top three producing tour operators are more adamant about their problems than their counterparts [$X^2 = 28.6$, DF = 8, Sig = 0.0004 and $X^2 = 29$, DF = 8, Sig = 0.0003 respectively]. In addition, the ones which are paid indirectly by tour operators (i.e., via incoming travel agencies), as well as the ones which accepted financial assistance in their construction and opening phases, had problems with tour operators more frequently than their counterparts [X^2 = 36.6, DF = 8, Sig = 0.00001 and X^2 = 12.1, DF = 4, Sig = 0.01 respectively]. This illustrates clearly that greater degrees of dependence generate conflicts. Although respondents verbally expressed a wide range of conflicts in their relation with tour operators, they probably feared declaring them directly.

Despite the unexpected low percentage of respondents suggesting that they had problems with tour operators, when asked to specify these conflicts, several issues were manifested. These conflicts resulted from the domination of tour operators in the tourism distribution channel, in combination with the marketing and management disadvantages of SMTEs and illustrated the severe implications for the competitiveness of hotels. The major hotel conflicts with tour operators are presented in Table 1.

Some hotel characteristics influence their ratings. Qualitative evidence confirms that *hotel location* plays an important role, as islands at different stages of their life cycle have dissimilar supply, resulting in varied relationships with tour operators. Hotels on developed islands face fierce local competition, which jeopardises their negotiation power with tour operators and generates a higher degree of conflicts. Hotels on developing islands tend to be more sensitive towards their occupancy and coverage of contracts in the low season, as they encounter greater seasonality. Qualitative evidence also

TABLE 1. Hotels' conflicts with tour operators

Conflicts	Mean	STD	95% confidence interval	
Prices as a problem with tour operator	4.386	1.014	4.265	4.507
Legal coverage is one sided, covering only tour operators	4.261	1.053	4.132	4.389
Tour operator's bankruptcies	4.260	1.170	4.116	4.403
Coverage of contracts	4.156	1.121	4.018	4.293
Misleading/direction of tourists to competing accommodation establishments	3.924	1.362	3.755	4.094
Payment delays	3.888	1.310	3.730	4.045
Request for high quality without payment	3.838	1.313	3.675	4.000
Late release of unwanted allocation	3.777	1.347	3.610	3.944
Accommodation allocation upon arrival	3.335	1.432	3.153	3.516

Notes: Likert Scale 1-5 (Very Unimportant–Very Important).

illustrates that when hotel proprietors *operate an incoming travel agency* as well, they tend to under-rate most of the conflicts with tour operators, as they can use their dual role to maximise their benefit and reduce conflicts.

4.1. Prices Charged by Hotels as an Area of Conflict with Tour Operators

The *price that hotels are forced to charge tour operators for their services* was the most important conflict from the hoteliers' point of view. As most SMTEs are unable to negotiate an acceptable price with major tour operators they are often forced to accept the proposed price. Fierce competition at the place of origin of the tourist and "price wars" force tour operators to sacrifice profit margins in order to maintain market share. As a result, hotels are often given little choice but to offer, or rather accept, predetermined contract prices which cover only the devaluation of a destination's currency and a fraction of the inflation at the place of origin, regardless of the local inflation, operational and capital costs. The inability of many SMTEs to calculate their costs accurately, as well as their lack of understanding of financial management effectively means that depreciation is not taken into account and the cost for renovations is not added to prices. Hence hotels fail to invest back to their property which makes them less attractive and pushes prices further down. Qualitative research confirmed that often prices offered by tour operators are below the variable operational cost and therefore hoteliers attempt to minimise their losses rather than maximise profit. Moreover, due to the marketing and management weaknesses of SMTEs, the inability of hotels to compete effectively in the global market reduces the possibilities to identify and utilise alternative distribution methods.

Interviewees explained that this is a chronic problem, which deteriorates gradually due to the concentration in the European tour operators industry, which increases their bargaining power. Buhalis (1995) illustrated that in 1993, Greek hotels in general had a negative profit margin (-7%), while their profitability was continuously decreasing, due to their inability to increase the prices in line with local inflation and operational costs. Several interviewees explained that their prices on tour operators' contracts have failed to increase for several years. This was despite the effects of inflation (about 15% at the time) and the cost of capital on their operational costs. They also emphasised that net prices in 1993 were cheaper in a foreign currency than 20 years earlier and several properties were forced into liquidation. They also stressed that smaller hotels which received greater pressures for lower prices could survive only because of the personal efforts and unpaid employment of proprietors' families.

In addition, interviewees emphasised that tour operators force prices down across all accommodation categories. Hence, higher category establishments offer similar prices to one star hotels, which provide only a fraction of the services and facilities and thus have much less investment requirements and operational costs. Interviewees expressed very strong feelings against tour operators' practices, which they believe "blackmail" and "blood-suck" them, while they "treat them as slaves." Finally, they illustrated that price negotiations with tour operators have become so drastic lately that they had direct impacts on the quality of their services, as tour operators often suggest the "reduction of the linen change weekly or even the toilet paper provided" in order to reduce prices.

An analysis of the *average annual increase in tour operators' contract rates* was examined in order to examine the foundations of this conflict. Only 6.3% of the respondents managed to attract an annual average increase in their prices above 15% during the period 1990-1993, despite a 16.6% average annual inflation rate and higher operational cost increases. The majority (63.6%) achieved an average of less than 10%, illustrating the accumulated loss they face and their inability to maintain the quality of their services. *Lower category and smaller properties* suffered from this problem more severely, as they attracted lower increases [$X^2 = 18.2$, DF = 12, Sig = 0.1, and R = 0.22, Sig = 0.0004]. Related with the size and category of hotels, their marketing budget plays a significant role in the annual increase of contract prices. Properties with higher *marketing budgets* achieved higher price increases, confirming the argument that SMTEs' strategic weaknesses and low channel power result from their marketing and management disadvantages.

Not surprisingly, the *distribution mix* is another issue which influences the achieved prices on tour operators' contracts. The more tour operators they co-operate with, the more likely hotels are to accomplish a higher price increase [R = 0.25, Sig = 0.00006], as they spread their capacity to several partners and markets and therefore diminish their dependence. Similarly, the *hotel allocation to the first and top three producing tour operators* plays an instrumental role in their ability to increase their prices. The higher the allocation hotels offer to the first and top three producing tour operators, the less the price increase they are likely to achieve [R = -0.24, Sig = 0.0002 and R = -0.15, Sig = 0.02 respectively], reinforcing the implications of the dependence on prices. Moreover, the *qualifications of respondents*, as well as their *job title* were reflected on the increase of prices achieved. Expectedly, better qualified respondents had more marketing skills, and therefore could negotiate better and reject unprofitable contracts, achieving higher price increases. The ability of *managers* to attract better prices from tour operators than *owners* can be a result of several factors. Not only do managers tend to be employed in larger and higher category properties, but also they are often better qualified, as they are obliged by law to hold certain educational and professional qualifications. Understandably, the higher the *average annual price increase* on tour operators' contracts, the more *satisfied respondents* were with their operations [R = 0.37, Sig = 0.0].

The *number of tour operators co-operating* with each hotel influences the rating of the price conflict. The fewer tour operators co-operating with a hotel, the higher this conflict was rated [R = −0.11, Sig = 0.07]. Also the higher *the allocation offered to the first and top three producing tour operators*, the higher respondents rated the price conflict with tour operators [R = 0.11, Sig = 0.08 and R = 0.12, Sig = 0.07 respectively]. Although statistically significant, these correlations are not strong. Interviewees provided qualitative evidence confirming these inferences. Interestingly, properties which do not co-operate with tour operators rated the price problem indifferently as a "very important" one. This is a result of their previous experiences, which have forced them either to cease or never to initiate co-operation with tour operators. Naturally, the rating of this problem depended on the *annual price increase to tour operators*, as there was a low negative relationship between the price increase achieved and the rating of this conflict [R = −0.19, Sig = 0.002]. The price dispute was also reflected in *hotels' satisfaction with their performance*, as the lower the rating of the price conflict with tour operators, the higher their satisfaction with their performance [R = −0.27, Sig = 0.00001]. Personal characteristics of the respondents also affected their perception of the price problem. For example, their *job title* influenced their rating, as owners tend to rate this conflict higher than managers [X^2 = 14.3, DF = 4, Sig = 0.006], perhaps due to the characteristics of the properties they represent. In addition, there was a weak correlation between these conflicts and their *academic qualifications*, which was also supported by qualitative analysis. Less qualified respondents rated the price problem higher than better qualified ones. This is due to their relatively lower ability to negotiate with tour operators or to identify alternative ones, as well as by the fact that better qualified respondents are normally employed in larger and higher category properties.

Evidently therefore the strategic weaknesses of SMTEs are greatly responsible for the difficulties they face in achieving adequate price increases in their contracts with tour operators. The size and types of hotel, the hotel category, marketing budget, distribution mix and the qualifications of decision makers were identified as statistically significant variables and determined their ability to negotiate annual price increase on their contracts with tour operators. Smaller properties suffered the consequences more severely, as they could not achieve adequate price increases on tour operators' contracts and consequently were driven by the "down-ward/pessimistic quality cycle," effectively deteriorating their profitability yearly.

Interviewees elaborated on *nine techniques tour operators use to suppress their prices*, as illustrated in Figure 2. They argued that a wide range of techniques are being used which aim to control the desirability and demand for particular destinations and properties, in order to keep prices down. First, as tour operators finalise their contracts more than one year before the arrival of their customers (typically they sign contracts in July for the following summer season) the (1) *timing of negotiating contracts* plays an important role in the bargaining power of each partner. If a particular year is forecasted to be rather good for a destination, i.e., a healthy level of bookings is expected, tour operators try to withhold information about bookings and negotiate hotel contracts for the next year quite early, during the low period. This enables them to capitalise on hoteliers' agony for the current season and to persuade them easily to drop prices in order to stimulate demand. If negotiations are postponed and hoteliers enjoy a "good season" they would be confident and thus reluctant to reduce their prices. In contrast, when a year is predicted to hold low demand for a destination, tour operators attempt to negotiate contracts later during the season, in order to take advantage of hotels' disappointment and their inclination to offer special offers for last minute bookings. Hoteliers claim that once they have agreed the contracts for the next year, the real booking situation is presented to them by tour operators.

Secondly, interviewees claimed that tour operators often use their (2) *customer satisfaction surveys* to ask for a further deduction on prices or special offers. In a monthly confidential report a variety of qualities are assessed, rated and ranked for all hotels used by tour operators in each destination. Several interviewees accused tour operators of altering the figures in order to argue that hotel services are incompetent and therefore, request better services (without increasing prices) or further price reductions. Should they disobey, hotels are threatened with their contract being cancelled for the next

FIGURE 2. Nine Techniques Used by Tour Operators in Order to Reduce Prices at Hotels

1. Timing of negotiating contracts-bargaining during low occupancy periods
2. Misquoting customer satisfaction surveys
3. Directing/Misleading tourists to certain properties
4. Short release period which does not allow adequate time for selling unused rooms
5. Over-contracting and renegotiating of prices after low coverage of contracts
6. Structural destination seasonality circle
7. Alter/misleading image for destinations and properties
8. Play hotels against each other
9. Oligopsony (few buyers) at destinations

season, while no last minute bookings are provided in the low season. These techniques are based on tour operators' expert and coercive power over hotels. Hotels are not in a position to know the real picture of their bookings while they are constantly threatened with cessation of co-operation or reduction of bookings. Hotels explained that power is also applied by (3) *directing tourists to certain properties*, often by untruthfully suggesting that their original property has no vacancies, is overbooked or even experiences a major problem and may be a health risk! This is often used in conjunction with the "timing of contracts" technique as explained earlier.

A very (4) *short release period*, typically one-two weeks for "allotment" contracts and not even one day for "commitment" contracts prevents hoteliers from knowing the booking situation until too late. This is often combined with (5) *over-contracting properties* and re-negotiation of prices after a low coverage of contracts in order to increase demand. As a consequence, hoteliers have inadequate time to search for alternative markets and in most cases cannot rent their rooms. This is explained further in paragraph 4.8 and it is closely linked with "last minute" discounts as described in paragraph 4.9. Hoteliers claimed that especially in the low season tour operators often withhold confirmed bookings until a "special last minute offer" is negotiated. Once this is achieved tour operators confirm bookings they already had received for months and they profit extra from the special deal, as they do not reduce the price for customers.

SMTEs and hotels compete globally and it seems that there is a new type of (6) *structural seasonality circle*, which occurs especially between Mediterranean destinations. This is the effect of exceeding supply in the world tourism industry. As these destinations are often regarded as substitutable by consumers, tour operators were accused by interviewees of rotating their promotional emphasis between destinations. Hoteliers claimed that tour operators regularly arrange for destinations to have "one (or two) good year(s) following a bad one." For example, tour operators may promote one particular destination for one year (such as Spain), next they may advertise Southern France and Italian destinations, while in the third year they probably recommend Greece, Cyprus and Turkey. Public relations and marketing techniques such as advertising, coverage by media, destination reports, programmes on activities or crime in an area, can (7) *alter destinations' image* and influence demand. In this manner tour operators ensure that a destination enjoys high demand only once every several years. Consequently, they can exercise their coercive and expert power in order to maintain their negotiation strength and achieve low contract price. Should demand for a destination increase, hotels can achieve a temporarily higher increase in price, which then results in a drop in demand and further price reductions over the next one or two seasons.

Tour operators also (8) *play hotels against each other* during the bargaining process for new contracts. They deliberately quote that higher quality hotels offer lower prices from those negotiated and thus pressurise smaller properties to reduce their price. As hoteliers compete locally and also have a confidentiality closure in their contract, they are unable to check the validity of this claim and are forced to further reduce their prices.

Interviewees suggested that tour operators often formulate "gentlemen's agreements" not to interfere in each others' relationships with local hotels, unless it becomes unavoidable. This is "price fixing" and hence against competition laws. This enables them to impose an (9) *oligopsony* (few buyers) and increase their power over hotels. Several examples were quoted of tour operators offering contracts with much better terms, once a contract with another tour operator was terminated, but never while the co-operation was still active.

The analysis clearly illustrates that hotels are trapped in a spiral, which results in deterioration of the product quality offered to tourists, reduction of consumers' willingness to pay and further price reductions over the following seasons. Smaller and lower category hotels, which co-operate with one or a few tour operators often suffer more severe implications. However, a few interviewees, often representing larger and higher category properties, highlighted their differentiation in this fatalistic approach and stressed that there is a way of reversing this spiral. An "optimistic cycle" of improving the quality, initially financed by some hotels improved customer satisfaction and increased their willingness to pay. As a result, hotels enhanced their negotiation power, improving their profitability. Pricing of tourism products is a pivotal issue in the relationship between tour operators and SMTEs. It affects the profitability and viability of SMTEs at the micro level, and it also determines the economic benefits and influences the competitiveness of destinations at the macro level.

4.2. One Sided Legal Coverage Only for Tour Operators

In addition, most hotel respondents felt that contracts and agreements are one-sided, offering *legal coverage only for tour operators*, and leaving them uncovered should tour operators fail to perform their obligations. As more than 80% rated this criterion "important" or "very important," there were few statistically significant relationships between hotel characteristics and their rating. However, qualitative research suggests that smaller and lower category properties face this problem more drastically, as they have no financial means and legal expertise. Thus, they feel powerless to pursue any dispute they have with tour operators through the legal system.

Not surprising it seems that properties co-operating with fewer tour operators overrated this conflict. Hotels which do not co-operate with any tour operators often quoted this conflict as the major reason for not attempting to do so. The more *dissatisfied* respondents were with their financial performance, the more unprotected they felt [R = -0.23, Sig = 0.0002]. Naturally owners, in comparison with managers rated this problem higher than their colleagues [X^2 = 7.3, DF = 4, Sig = 0.1]. This is not only because they probably represented more vulnerable hotels, but also because they had a greater marketing and management illiteracy and therefore, were more reluctant to take risks and have a more aggressive distribution attitude.

4.3. Tour Operators' Bankruptcies

Closely related and almost equally rated with the above issue is the *"tour operator's bankruptcy"* conflict, which was often characterised as "nightmare." Once a tour operator is forced into liquidation, hotels are some of the last recipients of compensation after consumers and other legal bodies. This is in spite of the fact that they may have already delivered their products and services. Liquidations of major tour operators occur frequently and as they normally have very little assets, most hotels lose significant amounts of money. As they cannot afford to follow the legal procedures, losing money through a tour operator's bankruptcy is almost inevitable. Consequently there was a consensus among respondents on this issue and few differences according to their property characteristics. However, there was a negative relationship between the *capacity of hotels* and the rating of this conflict [R = -0.12, Sig = 0.06]. This illustrates that smaller properties tend to rate this conflict higher, as they often formulate agreements (and "commitments") with unknown and more risky tour operators. A tour operator bankruptcy may result in a loss equivalent to their revenue for one or two seasons.

Qualitative research illustrates that almost 20% of the respondents had at some stage lost large amounts of money from bankrupt tour operators. Liquidation of a tour operator has severe implications for hotels' future revenue and ability to fill their rooms for the next season, as they need to re-contract the unexpectedly available allocation to other tour operators, often at the last minute. Usually, new tour operators step in to acquire the available capacity, but often they are prepared to pay only a fraction of the original contract prices, as they realise that hotels are desperate to find new partners and hence have no bargaining power. Thus, tour operator bankruptcy has severe implications, not only for payments due, but also for the occupancy levels and profitability in the next years.

4.4. Coverage of Tour Operators' Contracts

The coverage of tour operators' contracts (i.e., the actual bookings vs. the contract reservations) was also rated consistently above the "important" line, due to its contribution to the occupancy levels of hotels during the low season. As hoteliers offer special rates, based on the assumption and promise that an appropriate coverage or occupancy level will be accomplished on the allocation of each tour operator, achieving these levels is vital for trouble-free co-operation between the two partners. Qualitative analysis however illustrates that tour operators tend to under-utilise their allotment in the low season and overuse it in the high season, causing low occupancy and over-booking respectively.

Firstly, an examination of the *actual average contract coverage levels* needs to be undertaken in order to assess which type of properties face a greater problem. The *larger the hotel*, the higher the level of actual coverage of their contract they manage to achieve [R = 0.19, Sig = 0.006]. This can be a result of the ability of larger properties to re-allocate allotments to other tour operators, should some of them be unproductive, and thus increase the average contract coverage. This hypothesis can be confirmed as the more *tour operators co-operate with a hotel*, the better the actual average contract coverage was achieved [R = 0.2, Sig = 0.003]. Moreover, there was a positive relationship between *the marketing budget of hotels* and their ability to achieve high contract coverage [R = 0.19, Sig = 0.02]. *Manager respondents* achieved better coverage of contracts in comparison with *owners* [X^2 = 17.3, DF = 4, Sig = 0.001], while the higher the *academic qualifications* of respondents, the higher the contract coverage they managed [X^2 = 35.9, DF = 20, Sig = 0.02]. This is perhaps as a result of more capable and qualified managers being employed in larger properties.

Tour operators often argue that should a *hotel increase prices* above the industry average, it would suffer from low demand and therefore low coverage of allotment. However, there was evidence that hotels with minimal annual increases in prices suffer equally from low coverage. Therefore, it can be concluded that the price does not necessarily determine demand and tour operators' contract coverage. Instead, offering value for money and quality at every price level determine the contract coverage.

The coverage of tour operators' contracts is also rated as a major source of conflict. *Larger hotels* rated this problem quite higher than their counterparts, as they normally depend on tour operators for almost all their clientele during the low season. In addition, they felt pressurised to cover their operational costs. In contrast, smaller and often family-run hotels underrated this problem as they do not need to pay for under-employed personnel (family). Moreover, as smaller and lower category properties and especially apartments, formulate "commitment contracts" they are paid by tour operators, regardless of the occupancy achieved. Therefore, in the short term, smaller hotels can in fact benefit from low contract coverage, both from reducing the variable costs and also by "double selling" their rooms to new customers.

However, they lose revenue from the food and beverage departments, as well as any additional services offered. In the long term, low coverage of the contract is interpreted as low desirability for the property and results in a reduction of negotiation power, and perhaps in prices in the following seasons. Several interviewees claimed that even in commitment contracts tour operators tend to request a re-negotiation during the same season, should they fail to cover their allocation.

Interviewees suggested that low coverage of tour operator contracts results from over-contracting. They explained that the practice is followed by tour operators in order to cover unpredictable high demand as well as to increase their bargaining power with hotels. Tour operators often contract up to 150% of their aircraft capacity in order to have the flexibility to re-adjust their operation, should a demand increase occur. Although tour operators have a clear indication of the bookings level by March, they keep their accommodation allocation until their release period. Interviewees also emphasised that although the Greek law gives hoteliers the right to reduce tour operators' allotments in the high season, should they fail to provide a reasonable coverage in the low season, this practice is very rarely followed. Hotels fear confrontation with their channel partners, as well as the penalties over the following years. Only a very small percentage (8%) of competent respondents quoted that should tour operators fail to provide sufficient coverage of their allotment, they would refuse to renew their contracts for the next season, indicating that the vast majority of hotels have a fatalistic attitude when designing their distribution mix. In contrast, most respondents believed that a certain degree of overbooking is inevitable in order to resolve this problem.

Furthermore, about 12% explained that in the past tour operators have cancelled contracts a few months before the arrival of consumers, without paying any compensation. This does not only occur on allotment contracts, where tour operators have no financial obligations if they do not provide customers, but also on commitment contracts, where tour operators have total control of the property and clearly undertake the entire risk for the season. This practice is fairly unusual and normally follows unforeseen events such as the Gulf War or tour operators' bankruptcy. However, several tour operators cancelled a contract at the last minute, simply because they could use cheaper properties or because they could forecast a lower demand than originally expected. This practice may result in financial disaster, especially for smaller hotels which often depend on one or a few tour operators for their entire clientele and revenue. They are forced to find alternative ways to distribute their products at the last minute, but often incoming travel agencies or other tour operators take advantage of their anxiety and gain enormous discounts, damaging their profitability.

4.5. Misleading/Directing Customers to Particular Tourism Enterprises

The issue of misleading consumers to particular tourism enterprises was emphasised by respondents. They suggested that tour operators are keen to fill their allocation in certain hotels first. These are normally properties on commitment contracts; properties which still negotiate a larger allotment and try to reduce rates; and finally, hotels which offer greater profit margins, especially through "last minute" deals. Interviewees claimed that tour operators divert demand towards these preferred properties by manipulating their presentation in brochures. They also claimed that tour operators often quote that the consumers' original accommodation choice is sold out or over-booked, and there is no more availability. This can happen when tourists attempt to book their holidays at an outgoing travel agency or even upon arrival. As compensation levels for changes effectively are minimal tour operators can easily convince most holidaymakers that a "little swap" is essential, due to unforeseen reasons, without affecting their holidays. For example, maximum £40 for Airtours and £50 for Owners Abroad, in 1994, if customers were notified in 0-14 and 0-7 days respectively, for change to an *inferior* standard accommodation. Often the problem appears at the last min-ute, travel agencies blame hoteliers and customers are happy to accept any alternative accommodation that is available at the time in order not to miss their holiday slot. About 10% of the interviewees repeatedly claimed that their loyal clients, who had enjoyed their one particular hotel and even for-mulated friendships with proprietors and personnel, have been forced to accept alternative accommodation or to miss their holidays. When they vis-ited their preferred hotel they often found that their original choice had plenty of availability and they felt deceived.

Evidently, the misleading problem was emphasised by lower *category properties*, while "A"' and "Lux" category hotels, as well as "apartments" rated this problem as less important. In the first case, high category hotels are not easily replaceable, as they have their clientele and distinctive product. On the other side, "apartments" normally benefit from this practice as they have a priority in bookings, due to "commitment" contract. This was supported by the negative relationships between the *percentage of hotels offered on a commit-ment basis* as well as the *allocation to the top producing tour operators* and the rating of this conflict [R = −0.26, Sig = 0.00003 and R = −0.24, Sig = 0.0002 respectively]. Moreover, there was a positive relationship between hotels' rating of the *need to increase co-operation at the destination* and the mislead-ing of customers as a conflict [R = 0.22, Sig = 0.0004]. This is attributed to the fact that respondents who highlighted this problem supported greater co-operation at the local level.

As tourists tend to formulate personal relationships with proprietors in smaller properties, they are the ones who emphasised this conflict with tour operators. This technique is also followed for entire destinations as well, and demonstrates the power of tour operators on the clientele and profitability of hotels. Interviewees suggested that when consumers made inquiries to tour operators for the reasons of misinformation, they were quoted that "although the property had some availability, there was no space on the charter flights," underlying the problem of over-contracting. There were also examples of prospective tourists asking for availability in one particular country, during the low period, only to be told that the entire destination is either sold out or unavailable. They are normally being directed to alternative destinations which experienced a low demand or would contribute more to the profitability of tour operators.

4.6. Delays in Payment

Tour operators earn for up to 25% of their profit margins on interest gained. Despite being paid well before consumers arrive at the destinations, the industry norm is to settle bills two weeks after clients' departure. Several interviewees claimed that their payments were delayed as long as one year. Usually, local incoming/handling travel agencies are in the middle of the dispute. They are accused by hoteliers of withholding money for a period of time in order to benefit from the interest and for improving their cash flow. This problem was experienced to a greater extent by smaller properties, as they have less bargaining power to request a prompt settlement than their counterparts. However, no statistically significant relationship between hotel characteristics and the rating of this conflict could be established.

4.7. Request for High Quality Without Appropriate Payment

Frequently, hoteliers accused tour operators of demanding unrealistically high quality products, despite their reluctance to pay adequately. This conflict was slightly overrated by *higher category and larger properties*, which offer a very wide range of facilities and services, as they were constantly asked to be requested to improve quality. In addition, there is a positive relationship between the ratings of the *need to increase co-operation* at the destination level and the ones for this conflict [R = 0.2, Sig = 0.001], highlighting that hotels regard closer local co-operation as a way to provide a better quality service. As expected, there was a low negative correlation between the *development of hotels' relations with tour operators* and this conflict [R = −0.14, Sig = 0.03], illustrating that this conflict contributes to the disputes between the two partners.

4.8. Late Release of Unwanted Accommodation Allocation

Late release of unwanted hotels' allocation is another conflict observed between hoteliers and tour operators. Most allotment contracts have a "release period," which obliges properties to accept bookings by a tour operator until one or two weeks prior to customer arrival, while preventing them from accepting reservations from alternative channels and independent travellers. Although tour operators may have a confirmed booking for one particular property, hotels are not normally notified until the release period. This conflict is closely related to the "coverage of tour operators' contracts" problem (see paragraph 4.4).

Should tour operators fail to cover their allocations hotels are unable to find customers at the last moment and often are left with unoccupied rooms, jeopardising their profitability. Several interviewees accused tour operators of using the late release option in order to enhance their leadership in the distribution channel. Tour operators can also withhold reservations in order to either divert demand to alternative properties providing better profit margins, or re-negotiate for further last minute discount with the hotel. Capitalising on hoteliers' agony in periods when they have low occupancy rates, minimal opportunities to sell their rooms elsewhere, and few reservations for the next weeks, tour operators often explain to hotels that their property "is not selling well." Then they are asked to reduce their prices again and to provide special offers in order to stimulate the very price-sensitive "last minute" market. Interviewees explained that once hotels reduce their prices, tour operators almost "magically" supply "healthy" booking lists of customers, who most probably had reserved their holidays well in advance. In this way, tour operators increase their profit margins, while ensuring further price discounts for the next seasons.

This conflict was emphasised by *smaller and lower category hotels*. In contrast, "apartments" are often contracted on a "commitment basis" and thus under-rated this conflict because they get paid regardless of whether their rooms are used. There was also some qualitative evidence demonstrating that very large hotels were less concerned about this conflict, as they could re-allocate rooms to other co-operating tour operators or use other channels and maximise their occupancy. Moreover, *respondents' title* influenced the rating of this conflict. *Owners* rated it higher than *managers* [$X^2 = 8.4$, DF = 4, Sig = 0.07], perhaps because they often represent a smaller hotel which co-operates with fewer tour operators. Interestingly, there was a negative correlation between *the annual tour operator price contract increase* and the rating of this conflict [$R = -0.19$, Sig = 0.004], illustrating that hotels which manage to achieve a higher price increase suffer less from the late release problem. This can only be interpreted as properties which offer appropriate services, build a strong reputation, and therefore can attract both higher price increases and also enjoy intentional demand. Also a negative relationship between the *development of hotels' relation with tour operators* and this conflict [$R = -0.2$, Sig = 0.002], illustrated that the higher respondents rated this conflict, the more they suggest that their relation with tour operators deteriorates.

4.9. Accommodation Allocation upon Customers' Arrival

Closely related with the above conflict, as well as the coverage of tour operators' contracts, is the "accommodation allocation upon consumers' arrival" as a problem. Interviewees attributed this practice to the attempts by tour operators to re-negotiate prices at the last minute and to direct tourists to where their commercial interests lie. Respondents claimed that this practice reduced consumers' awareness of the tourism product and region; increased their ignorance; diminished the importance attributed to the local culture and history; and caused irregularities and operational problems for hotels. They also claimed that tourists suffer from this practice as well, since they are normally allocated to inferior quality accommodation.

Evidently, this conflict was rated highly by lower category hotels, which are normally provided by allotment contracts. The more the *allocation to the top producing tour operator*, as well as the higher the *percentage offered on a commitment contract*, the lower this conflict is rated [R = -0.18, Sig = 0.006 and R = -0.25, Sig = 0.0001 respectively]. This suggests that smaller properties and apartments which are distributed through few tour operators, often on commitment contract, can enjoy a boost in their occupancy at the last moment and thus, they underrated this problem. Naturally, the rating of the *tour operator relations development* is negatively related with the rating of this conflict [R = -0.18, Sig = 0.005], demonstrating that hoteliers who believed that there was an improvement in their relation with tour operators underrated this conflict. Finally, there was a slight positive correlation between the rating of the *need to increase co-operation at the destination* and the rating of this conflict [R = 0.16, Sig = 0.01], illustrating that respondents may regard local co-operation as a way to reduce this problem.

4.10. Change of Relationship with Tour Operators over the Years

In order to examine hoteliers' perception on the overall development of their relationships with tour operators over the last five years, a Likert Scale (1-5: Much Worse-Much Better) was employed. Responses reflected their disappointment which was evident in the qualitative analysis, as on average they believed that their relation deteriorated (mean = 2.18, STD = 1.08). Some 33.2% of the respondents believed that the situation was becoming "much worse," while 32.9% rated it as "worse." Moreover, 17.7% reported that the situation is "stable" while only 15.2% could see an "improvement," and a further 0.7% declared a "big improvement."

Lower category properties emphasised that their relationship with tour operators and their negotiation power deteriorated constantly, while *higher category hotels and "apartments"* were slightly more optimistic. This can be interpreted as a result of the high quality facilities offered by higher category hotels as well as the demand for self-catering accommodation, which effectively increased the competitiveness and inter-channel power of "these categories." Understandably, there was a fairly strong negative correlation between the majority of the aforementioned conflicts and the rating of the development of hotels' relationship with tour operators. Naturally, the higher the *price conflict* was rated, the worse the development of the relation was assessed [R = 0.31, Sig = 0.0]. This was also confirmed as, the higher the *discount that was offered by hotels in allotment contracts in the low and high season as well as on commitment contracts*, the worse they rated the development of their relationship with tour operators [R = −0.15, Sig = 0.09; R = −0.17, Sig = 0.05 and R = −0.29, Sig = 0.06] respectively. Moreover, several other negative but lower correlations with other conflicts were evident: *"legal coverage is one sided"* [R = −0.17, Sig = 0.008], *"late release"* [R = −0.19, Sig = 0.002], *"coverage of contracts"* [R = −0.24, Sig = 0.0001], *"request of high quality without extra payment"* [R = −0.14, Sig = 0.03], and *"misleading of tourists"* [R = −0.14, Sig = 0.02]. Consequently the higher the rating conflicts with tour operators, the more respondents felt that the relationship between themselves and tour operators deteriorated.

There was also a trend for *newer hotels* to be more positive towards the developments in the relationship with tour operators [X² = 25.2, DF = 15, Sig = 0.05]. This is perhaps because tour operators tend to move from older properties to modern ones, which offer a better range of facilities, and thus enjoy a higher level of competitiveness. In addition, there was a low positive correlation between the *number of tour operators* in co-operation and the development in hotels' relationships with them [R = 0.12, Sig = 0.04]. This underlines that hotels which co-operate with a larger number of tour operators enjoy a stronger position. It also illustrates that larger and higher category hotels are in a more privileged position within the distribution channel. Finally, there was also a positive relationship between the change of relation with tour operators and the *level of hotels' satisfaction* by their performance [R = 0.33, Sig = 0.0]. Clearly hoteliers' relationship with tour operators is pivotal for their profitability and satisfaction. New methods should therefore be identified to enable a closer and better co-operation between the two partners.

5. A WORD OF CONCLUSION

This paper examines the under-researched area of relationships in the distribution channel of tourism. A brief introduction to the theoretical framework illustrates that distribution becomes one of the most significant elements of tourism marketing. The paper then concentrates on the conflict experienced in the distribution channel between hoteliers and tour operators in the Mediterranean summer/seaside resort context. The paper aims to illuminate this area, to identify significant variables for its assessment and to provide a solid background for further research on the topic.

In conclusion, the majority of hotels' conflicts with tour operators tend to concentrate on the profit margin they are allowed to gain, the occupancy and coverage of contracts, as well as the financial security of their co-operation. Evidently hoteliers rated these conflicts according to a number of factors, mainly their competitiveness in the distribution channel, as well as their dependence on the tour operators. In most cases respondents from larger and higher category hotels under-rated the aforementioned conflicts, due to their ability to amend their distribution mix in order to take advantage of alternative and more profitable tour operators, should their co-operation fail to yield satisfactory results. In addition, the differences between contract types also played a significant role in ratings. For example properties which are based on commitment contracts, such as "apartments," tend to underrate conflicts referring to occupancy, release periods and contract coverage. The number of tour operators a property co-operates with was often instrumental in the rating of conflicts, as it determined dependency. The more the tour operators in co-operation, the easier it is to re-engineer the distribution channel and therefore the lower the conflict levels were rated.

In addition, the stronger the competitive position a hotel gains, the less problems it encounters with tour operators, due to a more equal distribution of power within the channel. In contrast, easily replaceable, small, unsophisticated hotels which lack a wide range of required facilities tend to face a wide range of problems, on both occupancy and profit margin aspects. Should they fail to obey tour operator requirements, small properties can experience extensive coercive and expertness power from tour operators. Therefore, hotels are required to assess their strategic position, identify specific attributes which would enable them to differentiate their product, attract and satisfy niche markets and formulate co-operation schemes at the destination level. Closer collaboration and the utilisation of information technology would enable hoteliers to expand their distribution mix and to enhance their position in the distribution channel. Failing to do so will deteriorate their competitiveness, as globalisation and vertical integration in European tourism effectively means that they will have an even smaller number of larger and more powerful tour operators to deal with in the future. Collaboration and innovative use of information technology will facilitate the increase of the competitiveness of both individual hotels and destinations as a total (Buhalis, 1991, 1993, 1994 and 1995; Buhalis and Cooper 1998; Cooper and Buhalis, 1992). Hence they will be able to augment their power within the tourism distribution channel and gain tools which will allow them to overcome conflicts with tour operators and collaborate on a more equitable basis.

BIBLIOGRAPHY

Allen, T., 1985, Marketing by a small tour operator in a market dominated by big operators, European Journal of Marketing, Vol.19(5), pp. 83-90.

Baywater, M., 1992, The European tour operator industry, Special report No.2141, Economist Intelligence Unit, London.

Baywater, M., 1994, Who owns whom in the European travel trade, Travel and Tourism Analyst, No.3, pp. 73-92.

Baywater, M., 1997, The European travel agency industry, Research report, Travel and Tourism Intelligence Unit, London.

Beaver, A., 1993, Mind your own travel business: A manual of retail travel practice, Beaver Travel Publishers, England.

Bitner, M., and Booms, B., 1982, Trends in travel and tourism marketing: The changing structure of distribution channels, Journal of Travel Research, Vol.20(4), Spring, pp. 39-44.

Bote, G., Sinclair, T., 1991, Integration in the tourism industry: a case study approach, in Sinclair, T., and Stabler, M., (eds) The tourism industry: An international analysis, CAB International, Oxford, pp. 67-91.

Britton, S., 1989, Tourism, dependency and development: A mode of analysis, in Singh, T., Theuns, H., Go, F., (eds), Towards appropriate tourism: The case of developing countries, Peter Land, Frankfurt, pp. 93-116.

Buhalis, D., 1991, Strategic marketing and management for the small and medium tourism enterprises in the periphery of the European Periphery: A case study of the Aegean Islands, Greece, MSc dissertation, Department of Management Studies for Tourism and Hotel Industries, University of Surrey.

Buhalis, D., 1993, Regional integrated computer information reservation management systems as a strategic tool for the small and medium tourism enterprises, Tourism Management, Vol.14(5), pp. 366-378.

Buhalis, D., 1994, Information and telecommunications technologies as a strategic tool for small and medium tourism enterprises in the contemporary business environment, in Seaton, A., et al. (eds), Tourism–The state of the art, J., Wiley and Sons, England, pp. 254-275.

Buhalis, D., 1995, The impact of information telecommunications technologies upon tourism distribution channels: Strategic implications for small and medium sized tourism enterprises' management and marketing," PhD dissertation, Department of Management Studies, University of Surrey.

Buhalis, D., and Cooper, C., 1998, Competition or co-operation: Small and Medium sized Tourism Enterprises at the destination, in E. Laws, B. Faulkner, G. Moscardo, (ed.), Embracing and managing change in Tourism, Routledge, London, pp. 324-346.

Christopher, M., 1986, The strategy of distribution management, Aldershot Gower, London.

Christopher, M., 1991, Distribution and Customer Service, in Baker, M. (ed), The Marketing Book, 2nd ed., London: Butterworth-Heinemann, pp. 378-383.

Cooper, C., and Buhalis, D., 1992, Strategic management and marketing of small and medium sized tourism enterprises in the Greek Aegean islands, in Teare, R.,

Adams, D., and Messenger, S., (eds), Managing projects in hospitality organisations, Cassell, London, pp. 101-125.

Gattorna, J., 1990, (ed), The Gower handbook of logistics and distribution management, 4th ed., Gower, England.

Gee, C., Makens, J., and Choy, D., 1989, The travel industry, 2nd ed., Van Nostrand Reinhold, New York.

Holloway, C., 1998, The business of tourism, 5th ed., Addison Wesley Longman, London.

Howitt, S., 1995, Travel Agents and Overseas Tour Operators, Keynote, London.

Josephides, N., 1993, Managing tourism in a recession, Tourism Management, Vol.14(3), pp. 162-166.

Josephides, N., 1994, Tour operators and the myth of self regulation, Tourism in Focus, Tourism Concern, No.14, Winter, pp. 10-11.

Laws, E., 1997, Managing Packaged Tourism, Thomson Business Press, London.

Middleton, V., 1994, Marketing in travel and tourism, 2nd Butterworth-Heinemann, London.

Mill, P., and Morrison, A., 1985, The tourism system: an introductory text, Prentice Hall International Editions, New Jersey.

Monopolies and Mergers Commission, 1986, Foreign package holidays, Presented to Parliament by the Secretary of State for Trade and Industry, HMSO, London.

Monopolies and Mergers Commission, 1989, Thomson Travel Group and Horizon Travel Ltd: A report on the merger situation, Presented to parliament by the Secretary of State for Trade and Industry by Command of her Majesty, CM554, HMSO, London.

Monopolies and Mergers Commission, 1997, Foreign package holidays, Presented to Parliament by the Secretary of State for Trade and Industry, HMSO, London.

O'Brien, K., 1996, The West European Leisure Travel Market, Financial Times Newsletters and management reports, London.

Ottaway, M., 1992, Turtle power, The Sunday Times, Travel and Style, 28 June.

Renshaw, M., 1997, The travel agent, 2nd ed., Centre for travel and tourism, Business Education Publishers Ltd, Sunderland.

Renshaw, M., 1994, Consequences of integration in UK tour operating, Tourism Management, Vol.15(4), pp. 243-245.

Roekaerts, M., and Savat, K., 1989, Mass tourism in South and Southeast Asia–a challenge to Christians and the churches, in Singh, T., Theuns, H., Go, F., (eds), Towards appropriate tourism: the case of developing countries, Peter Land, Frankfurt, pp. 35-69.

Shaw, G., and Williams, A.M., 1994, Critical issues in tourism: a geographic perspective, Blackwell, Oxford.

Sheldon, P., 1994, Tour operators, in Witt, S., and Moutinho, L., (eds), Tourism marketing and management handbook, 2nd ed., Prentice Hall, London, pp. 399-403.

Sinclair, T., Alizadeh, P., Onunga, E., 1992, The structure of international tourism and tourism development in Kenya, in Harrison, D., (ed), Tourism and the less developed countries, Belhaven Press, London, pp. 47-63.

Stern, L., and El-Ansary, A., 1992, Marketing channels, 4th ed., Prentice Hall, New Jersey.

Valenzuela, M., 1991, Spain: the phenomenon of mass tourism, in Williams, A., and Shaw, G., Tourism and economic development: Western European experiences, 2nd ed., Belhaven Press, pp. 40-60.

Wanhill, S., 1998, Intermediaries, in Cooper, C., Fletcher, J., Gilbert, D., Sheppard, R., and Wanhill, S., (eds), Tourism: principles and practice, 2nd ed., Addison Wesley Longman, London.

Welburn, H., 1987, Travel selling and distribution–new technology and trends in Europe, Travel and Tourism Analyst, July, pp. 3-15.

WTO, 1975, Distribution channels, World Tourism Organisation, Madrid.

The Effect of Cross-Industry Cooperation on Performance in the Airline Industry

Darla J. Domke-Damonte

SUMMARY. Airline services are one part of the inter-connected network of travel services. Brandenburger and Nalebuff (1995, 1996) suggested that firms may add value to their offerings by cooperating with other members of a firm's value net (competitors, substitutors, customers, and suppliers). In a 14-year longitudinal study, this paper explores the evolution of cooperative relationships between members of the U.S. domestic airline industry and other firms outside the U.S. domestic airline industry, with the goal of identifying performance effects associated with such cooperative alliances. Results of the pooled, cross-sectional time series regression indicate that cooperative alliances outside the U.S. airline industry contribute positively to performance when environments are rapidly changing and variable. *[Article copies available for a fee from The Haworth Document Delivery Service: 1-800-342-9678. E-mail address: getinfo@haworthpressinc.com <Website: http://www.haworthpressinc.com>]*

KEYWORDS. Cooperation, performance, airline industry, competition

Much of the literature on competitive strategy has focused on how firms seek to develop advantage over their competitors by maintaining secrecy of their actions in order to preempt competitive actions taken by competitors (Scherer, 1970; Kwandwalla, 1981; Smith, Grimm, Gannon, & Chen, 1991).

Darla J. Domke-Damonte is affiliated with the E. Craig Wall Sr. School of Business Administration, Coastal Carolina University, Conway, SC 29582-6054 (e-mail: ddamonte@coastal.edu).

[Haworth co-indexing entry note]: "The Effect of Cross-Industry Cooperation on Performance in the Airline Industry." Domke-Damonte, Darla J. Co-published simultaneously in *International Journal of Hospitality & Tourism Administration* (The Haworth Press, Inc.) Vol. 1, No. 1, 2000, pp. 141-160; and: *Global Alliances in Tourism and Hospitality Management* (ed: John C. Crotts, Dimitrios Buhalis, and Roger March) The Haworth Press, Inc., 2000, pp. 141-160. Single or multiple copies of this article are available for a fee from The Haworth Document Delivery Service [1-800-342-9678, 9:00 a.m. - 5:00 p.m. (EST). E-mail address: getinfo@haworthpressinc.com].

More recent work has identified the importance of considering cooperative, inter-firm collaboration as a useful tool to understand strategic action (Gulati, 1995; Ingram & Inman, 1996; Jarillo, 1988; Nielsen, 1988; Powell, Koput, & Smith-Doerr, 1996; Thorelli, 1986). Cooperative actions provide firms with an ability to reduce unexpected behavior by other firms by increasing the perceived interdependence.

However, while these research articles lend attention to the competitive advantages to be gained by general cooperation with other firms, they do not give explicit attention to the role of cooperative associations outside the focal industry. In fact, Gulati (1995) notes that research attention is needed to consider the effects of cross-industry cooperative alliances on firm outcomes. For example, cooperative relationships within the hospitality and tourism environment are growing, as evidenced by the increasing visibility of cooperative relationships internationally between airlines, hotels, restaurants, mortgage companies, rental car companies, credit card providers, and florists, among others. Referring to cooperative agreements with other airlines, Richard Stirland, director general of the Orient Airline Association, commented, "You lose focus if you are involved in anything up to a dozen different arrangements of varying scale and intensity, and your staff no longer really knows where that focus is" (Maxon, 1996: 1D).

It is also evident that such relationships place demands on firm resources that would otherwise be available for other applications. Nevertheless, at least alliances with other airlines have been suggested by Greg Brenneman, chief operating officer of Continental, to contribute as much as $20 million to the bottom line of the respective carrier (Maxon, 1996). As a result, it is critical to understand whether the benefits that firms realize from cooperative relationships outside their industry outweigh the costs of such activities. Given the attention focused on competition in the airline industry in the investigation of competitive strategies in previous research (Chen & MacMillan, 1992; Chen & Hambrick, 1995; Chen & Miller, 1994; Chen, Smith, & Grimm, 1992; Miller & Chen, 1994, 1996; Venkataraman, Chen, & MacMillan, 1997), this research tests the relationship between an airline company's intensity of use of cooperative relationships outside the U.S. domestic airline industry and its performance as measured by operating profit margin, OPM. The following sections provide a brief overview of the literature, the hypotheses tested within the study, the methods used to gather and analyze the data, and the results of the study.

LITERATURE REVIEW

Cooperative relationships have been referred to in many ways. Astley and Fombrun (1983: 578) referred to cooperative relationships as collective strategy, "the joint mobilization of resources and formulation of action within collectivities of organizations." Mitchell and Singh (1996: 170) described collaboration as ". . . cooperative agreements between legally separable organizations that do not involve establishing separate organizations." Das and Teng (1998: 492) referred to strategic alliances as "interfirm cooperative arrangements aimed at achieving the strategic objectives of the partners." Others (Buckley & Casson, 1988; Doz, 1996; Teece, 1992) emphasize the role of cooperation and trust in alliances.

The consistent focus in each of these definitions is the emphasis on how joint action between organizations enables them to compete by reducing uncertainty through increasing interdependence in what Aldrich and Whetten (1981) call the organizational action set, the "interacting group of organizations." Such cooperative inter-firm relationships serve as ". . . a mode of regulating interdependence between firms which is different from the aggregation of these units within a single firm and from coordination through market signals (prices, strategic [competitive] moves, tacit collusion, etc.) and which is based on a cooperative game with partner-specific communication"(Grandori & Soda, 1995: 184-185).

Thorelli (1986) suggested that cross-firm cooperation was an appropriate tool for managers of complex services. With the exception of Mitchell and Singh's (1996) study on survival of hospital software businesses as a function of cooperative relationships, much of the research on cooperative moves has been completed in the manufacturing sector (c.f., Gulati, 1995; Powell et al., 1996). Notable exceptions in the service sector include Provan's (1982) investigation of relationships to United Way funding for social service organizations and Ingram and Inman's (1996) study on cooperation among hotels on either side of Niagara Falls.

In each of these cases, it was cooperation with similar organizational types that was investigated. However, firms often cannot predict accurately the actions and reactions of competitors (Thompson, 1967), and therefore may use cooperative relationships to reduce the uncertainty in their product markets through information sharing and cross-firm communication in the form of cooperative relationships that range from cooperative marketing to pooled research and development cooperatives (Bresser, 1988; Oster & Pickrell, 1986). As a result, organizations may also compete within their organizational action set by joining up with other types of organizations for short-term or long-term relationships that provide synergies for the partners which can be used to compete effectively with others outside the cooperative arrangement (Brandenburger & Nalebuff, 1995, 1996).

Brandenburger and Nalebuff (1995) conceptualize strategic moves taken by the firm relative to four groups (Exhibit 1): groups linked vertically to the firm (customers and suppliers), and groups linked horizontally to the firm (complementors and substitutors). Brandenburger and Nalebuff (1995: 61)

EXHIBIT 1. Players in a Company's Value Net and Elements of the Cooperative Strategic Repertoire

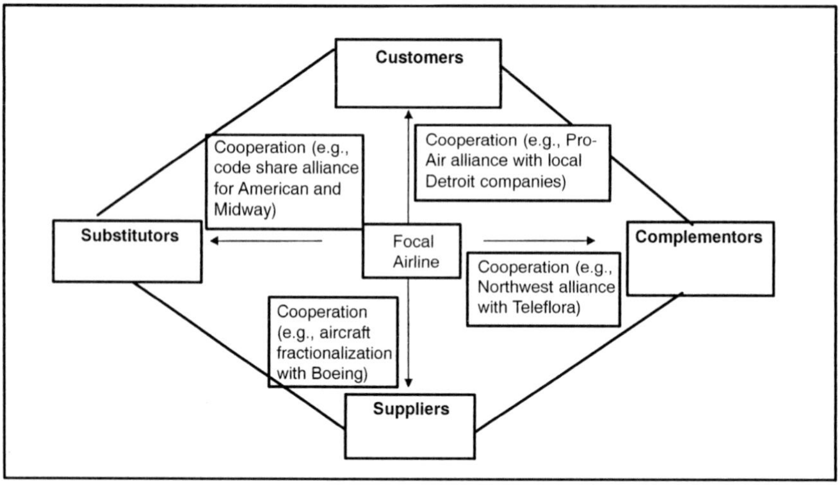

*Extension of Brandenburger and Nalebuff (1995).

define complementors as "players from whom customers buy complementary products or to whom suppliers sell complementary resources," and substitutors as "alternative players from whom customers may purchase products or to whom suppliers may also sell their resources." The interactive diagram depicted in Exhibit 1 clearly reflects the theoretical challenges faced by businesses producing complex goods (Mitchell & Singh, 1996), and the potential benefits associated with cooperative moves for such firms. More specifically, Mitchell and Singh (1996: 170) define complex goods as "an applied system with components that have multiple interactions and constitute a nondecomposable whole." Given that air travel plays a paramount role in the travel system, it is possible to view airline travel as embedded (Granovetter, 1985) as one part of a larger system in which airlines, hotels, cruise lines, rental cars, and travel agencies may all potentially interact (symbiotic interdependence) in a variety of combinations to produce a travel service. As a result, it is not inappropriate to consider that airline companies might choose cooperative cross-industry relationships to maximize their ability to provide a more apparently seamless service for the customers of the firm through any of the various types of interdependence.

For example, linking airline frequent flyer programs with hotels, restaurants, and rental car services, among others, adds value by creating switching costs between carriers for customers who need to continue to fly with the same airline to accumulate points applicable to rewards (Levine, 1987). Furthermore, Pfeffer and Nowak (1976) have shown that mergers and cooperative relationships most often occur between industries that exchange many resources. This finding is also mirrored by Browne, Toh and Hu (1995) who found that one of the reasons that airline frequent flyer programs are associated with hotels, restaurants, and credit cards is to exchange valuable purchasing information about their shared customers. Furthermore, researchers in the strategic marketing literature (Jaworski & Kohli, 1993; Kohli & Jaworski, 1990) have emphasized the importance to firm performance of such proactive market-oriented behavior with respect to current and potential competitors, customers, and interfunctional coordination. Therefore, cooperation with firms outside the focal industry may provide access to scarce resources, lowered marketing costs through sharing information on customers, and increased utilization rates. Using interorganizational relationships to reduce the costs of doing business has been cited as a rationale for such relationships in previous research (Ring & Van de Ven, 1994). Moreover, though they did not distinguish between intra-industry and cross-industry cooperation, Lado, Boyd, and Hanlon (1997) suggested that firms following collaborative rent seeking behavior (cooperating heavily with other firms) would recognize above-average rents. In consideration of the modes by which cross-industry cooperation enables firms to offset competition by bringing new and innovative value-adding, or cost-decreasing benefits to an airline firm, the following hypothesis is developed:

H_1: Higher performance will be associated with U.S. airline firms pursuing high intensity of cooperative relationships outside the U.S. domestic airline industry.

However, firms pursuing collaborative rent-seeking behavior with high cooperation and low competition focus on building trust and reciprocity between firms by combining resources and skills (Lado et al., 1997). Such firms might overcommit their resources and their managerial energies to too many cooperative relationships, and be unable to compete against attacks by other firms due to a learned inability to accept the inherent risk and uncertainty of unilateral competitive actions. Therefore, although this strategy may contribute to short-term advantage, the neglect paid to competitive actions may render the firm threatened in the long-term.

Moreover, in highly dynamic environments, the average performance of firms across the industry fluctuates dramatically (Dess & Beard, 1984). March (1991) suggested that firms must balance between exploiting old certainties and exploring new possibilities and that firms which successfully increase the variability of learning and outputs vis-à-vis their competitors will be more capable of generating sustainable competitive advantage. Therefore, it is not unreasonable to suggest that under highly dynamic environments, firm managers need to seek increasingly novel ways to explore the possibilities of competing within their environment. Miller and Chen (1996) found that airline firms pursuing a larger range of competitive actions performed better in periods of high uncertainty. Cooperative actions initiated with hotels, restaurants, credit card companies, charities, and other organizations may enable airline firms to change the basis of competition, to cut costs, or to cause customers to develop greater switching costs between carriers. Therefore, in the present study, environmental dynamism is proposed to moderate the relationship between intensity of cooperative moves outside the airline industry and organizational performance. The following hypothesis describes the form of this relationship:

H_2:   Environmental dynamism will moderate the relationship between intensity of cooperative moves outside the airline industry and organizational performance, such that intensity of cooperative moves outside the industry will be more positively associated with performance during periods of high environmental dynamism.

Environmental munificence enables the growth and survival of firms within a market because resources critical to firms' success are abundant (Castrogiovanni, 1991; Dess & Beard, 1984). Castrogiovanni (1991) explains the impact of munificence on organizational performance as the relationship between exploited and total capacity in the environment. "Prices associated with environmental resources provide some indication of the extent to which total capacity remains unexploited, therefore indicating opportunities for greater exploitation and these prices are reflected in industry performance measures" (Castrogiovanni, 1991: 558). When opportunities exist for airline firms to utilize a broad variety of methods to compete with other carriers, there is less direct competition between each of the respective carriers. As a result, price wars and advertising battles are minimized, leading to greater performance potential for all players in the marketplace.

H_3:   Environmental munificence is positively associated with organizational performance.

Environmental complexity reflects the number of effective competitors within the market (Adelman, 1969; Morrison & Winston, 1995). Scherer (1970) reviewed industrial organization studies in concentration and profitability, and with one exception, all of the studies indicated a positive link between industry concentration and performance. With many competitors in the marketplace, competitive prices are driven down to equilibrium prices, and organizations must compete aggressively to maintain share. With high concentration and fewer competitors, market leaders can dictate competitive conditions and command rents as desired. While it is possible for tit-for-tat gamesmanship to reduce revenues of players in even a highly concentrated market, e.g., Brandenburger and Nalebuff (1995) give examples from the automotive industry illustrating how competition in an environment of high concentration with two major players can reduce revenues of both players to below breakeven, large players with high resource commonality are assumed to generally cease such action before it so adversely affects performance (Chen, 1996). Therefore, a negative relationship between environmental complexity (low concentration) and organizational performance is proposed.

H_4:   Environmental complexity is negatively associated with organizational performance.

Furthermore, investment in and control of resources (absorbed slack), such as a computerized reservations system, enables the firm to selectively monitor and learn from strategies undertaken by competitors also using the resource (Fewer Airlines, 1992; Morrison & Winston, 1995). In this way, those firms with control of such a strategic resource may be able to anticipate and preempt strategic moves of competitors by introducing difficult to imitate hybrid strategies. At the same time, too high a level of absorbed slack buried in such activities as selling and administrative expenses, clearly would be associated with lower levels of performance since such overinvestment would reduce the firm's profit margin. Hearings in front of the U.S. Senate Committee on Governmental Affairs (Fewer Airlines, 1992) have alleged that computerized reservation systems have provided sponsoring airlines with unfair competitive advantage by managing screen layouts such that the sponsoring airline's fares are more accessible to booking agents than those of competitors. As a result, the following exploratory hypothesis is developed:

H_5:   Airline firms that maintain large, computerized reservation systems will be associated with higher organizational performance.

Firms within the commercial airline industry are continuously challenged to attain economies of scope and scale (Hurdle, Johnson, Joskow, Werden, & Williams, 1989). As a result, concerns about organizational performance must also address the issue of the size of the organization. Size confers institutional legitimacy on the organization (Baum, 1996) and may enable the firm to pursue a broader variety of strategies without repercussion by other players. Along with greater legitimacy, size also confers greater resource allocation and potentially a larger playing field upon which to guard the firm's position. For example, Chen and Hambrick (1995) found that smaller airlines attacked more quickly than larger airlines, but were less likely than larger airlines to respond when attacked by other airlines. The differences in the alternatives available to carriers is also obvious in the changes taking place in the airline industry in the last few years, in which there is a clear separation in the strategies of the major airline carriers, the largest in terms of revenue, who appear to be focusing more on globalization and long-haul (long-distance) flights and active competitive and cooperative strategies, from the strategies pursued by the regional carriers, who have concentrated on efficiency within their own regional markets, as well as on negotiating cooperative alliances with the majors. Given the importance attached to operating efficiencies in the airline industry, it is suggested that larger firms have the potential for greater economic returns.

H_6:   Organizational size will be positively associated with organizational performance.

METHODS

Data, Sampling Frame, and Unit of Analysis

The sample for the study included all airline carriers that (a) offered scheduled passenger service in the United States during the time period 1983-1996, and (b) were categorized by the United States Department of Transportation as certificated air carriers–"An air carrier holding a Certificate of Public Convenience and Necessity issued by the DOT to conduct scheduled services interstate . . . These carriers operate large aircraft (30 seats or more or a maximum payload capacity of 7,500 pounds or more)" (Department of Transportation, 1994: G-1). This sampling frame is important because this period includes three very different periods of industry development. More specifically, evidence presented in front of the U.S. Senate indicates a marked change in the Herfindahl concentration ratios for commercial airlines from 1000 in 1978, to 800 by 1984, to 1300 in 1991 (Fewer Airlines, 1992). Therefore, there appear to be at least three distinct periods of competition in the commercial airline sector after deregulation in 1978, a period of growth, followed by shakeout and consolidation, and then rebuilding under new organizations. By explicitly modeling the effects of environmental conditions, this study attempted to capture these differences, providing an extension beyond previous studies that have used time periods (e.g., 1980-1986 for Miller & Chen, 1994) which crossed differing industry environments. Selection of the sample was affected by several factors: (a) extensive entry and exit in the industry during this time period, (b) the methodological limitations of the pooled, cross-sectional time series analysis that requires no missing data for any of the firms for any years of the study period, and (c) the lack of availability and/or comparability of international airline performance measures. As a result, the cross-industry cooperative moves of the top ten firms in the U.S. airline industry that already existed in 1983 (America West began operations in 1983) and continued to exist beyond the end of 1996 were targeted. These ten focal firms included: Alaska Airlines, American, America West, Continental, Delta, Northwest, Southwest, TWA, United, and USAir.

Operationalization of the Variables

The Intensity of Cooperative Moves Outside the Domestic Airline Industry (ICOOPOUT) was operationalized by doing a content analysis of every issue of *Aviation Daily* between 1983 and 1996. Content analysis is a technique used to make valid inferences from data to their context (Krippendorff, 1980) and requires that a sampling unit of analysis, and relevant coding scheme be identified and validated prior to the collection of data. *Aviation Daily* has been found to be a valid source for reporting notable activities on the part of commercial airlines, and has been used for content analyses in previous studies in the airline sector (Chen et al., 1992; Chen & MacMillan, 1992; Chen & Miller, 1994; Chen & Hambrick, 1995; Miller & Chen, 1994,1996; Smith et al., 1991; Venkataraman et al., 1997).

The sampling unit for the content analysis was the cooperative move taken with a firm outside the U.S. domestic airline industry. As a part of a larger study, the researcher recorded every action mentioned in *Aviation Daily* that identified the name of the respective airline, provided a brief description of that action and the date of the action, and then assigned one of several codes (as appropriate) to the respective action. The coding categories considered in the present study included: (R) Promotion Alliance with Non-airlines and (W) Other Cooperative Action with Firms Outside the Airline Industry. (A full list of all coding categories is presented in Exhibit 2.)

The coding instructions were developed, with slight adaptation, from Miller and Chen (1994), who verified the content validity of their categories with industry experts. Item W was added to the list in the interest of the present study to represent a larger variety of potential cooperative activity that airlines may undertake with firms outside the industry, such as cooperative ground handling arrangements, agreements with labor unions, and non-promotional cooperation with hotels, rental car companies, and consumer goods companies. Both intra-rater and inter-rater reliability checks were done prior to the main data collection, and both indicated acceptable reliability. The intra-rate reliability on a test sample after a two-month interval was $\alpha = 1.00$, and the inter-rater reliability among two alternative raters trained to use the coding instructions was acceptable at .78 when corrected for chance using Cohen's kappa (Nitko, 1983). Disagreements between coders were discussed and the coding instructions amended to preclude alternative interpretations.

The reporting unit for the study was the intensity of cooperative moves

EXHIBIT 2. Complete Coding Categories for Content Analysis of *Aviation Daily*

(A)	Price Cut
(B)	Price Increase
(C)	New Promotion
(D)	Service Improvement
(E)	New Service
(F)	Daily Departures Increase
(G)	Daily Departures Decrease
(H)	Route Exit
(I)	Route Entry
(J)	Entry Price Cut
(K)	Special Fare Advertisement
(L)	Ticket Purchase Requirement
(M)	Frequent Flyer Program Initiation
(N)	Fare Structure Change
(O)	Acquisition of New Plane
(P)	Hub Creation
(Q)	Commission Rate Change for Travel Agents
(R)	Promotion Alliances with Non-airlines
(S)	Feeder Alliance
(T)	Cooperation with Another Domestic Airline
(U)	Cooperation with Foreign Airline
(V)	Intraindustry Merger or Acquisition
(W)	Other Cooperative Action not included in above categories

outside the domestic airline industry. As Miller and Chen (1994) note, some of these actions occur much less frequently than others. To control for this contingency, a total for each of the types of cooperative moves outside the industry was derived for each firm as the total of the normalized amounts of each type of action that the firm undertook. This calculation is consistent with that used by Miller and Chen (1994, 1996).

ICOOPOUT was calculated as $ICOOPOUT_{it} = \ln [((\Sigma z_{ijt})/\ln(RPM_t)) + 2)]$, where z = standardized score of $i = 1,2,3, .. 10$ certificated airlines, $j = 1,2,3, .. 6$ corresponding to number of moves of type R and W, and $t = 1,2, ... 14$ years (1983-1996), RPM is the revenue passenger miles flown by the airline in the respective year, and 2 represents a constant such that the natural log could be taken. Revenue passenger miles was included to adjust for the size of the respective airline and the inherent likelihood that larger carriers would be more likely to embark upon more of such moves.

Environmental munificence (EM) was operationalized as the unexploited capacity in the environment as suggested by Castrogiovanni (1991). More specifically, environmental munificence was operationalized as the percent growth in passenger revenues over the last year in the industry. This data was gathered from the Air Transport Association's *Annual Survey of the Scheduled Commercial Airline Industry.*

Environmental complexity (EC) was operationalized as the inverted average Herfindahl index for market concentration at the airports listed in the top thirty that were served by the respective airline. More specifically, this measure was calculated in three stages: (1) Concentration ratios were calculated for each of the top thirty airports based on number of passengers enplaned for each year with the following equation: $C_y = 1 - \Sigma (S_i/S_y)^2$, where C was the concentration ratio, S was airline passengers enplaned, i was airline i ($i = 1,2,3, .. i$) and y was airport ($y = 1,2,3 .. 30$); (2) Average concentration ratios were calculated for each airline (i) based upon the average concentration ratio at all of the airports represented in the top thirty that the respective airline served. The following equation was used: $C_{it} = \Sigma (C_{yt})/N_{yt}$, where C_{it} was the concentration ratio for airline i in year t, C_{yt} was the concentration ratio at airport y in year t, and N_{yt} was the number of the top thirty airports into which the respective airline flew in year t; and (3) the average concentration ratio for each airline was calculated as the inverse of the average Herfindahl measure, consistent with Adelman (1969) and Morrison and Winston (1995), to capture the concept of a numbers-equivalent measure of effective competitors faced by the respective airline in the respective year. Therefore, higher scores on EC reflected the incidence of a greater number of effective competitors in the top airports in which the firm competed in the respective year. Data necessary to complete these calculations were taken from the *Air Carrier Industry Scheduled Service Traffic Statistics* based upon the market shares of the top carriers in the top passenger-enplaning markets in the United States.

Environmental dynamism (ED) was operationalized as the industry volatility of sales, represented by the standard deviation in growth in passenger revenues over the previous three years. This data came from the Air Transport Association's *Annual Survey of the Scheduled Commercial Airline Industry*. The interaction between Intensity of Cooperative Moves Outside the Airline Industry (ICOOPOUT) and Environmental Dynamism (ED) was calculated by postmultiplying the values of each of the respective variables after each had been standardized by subtracting its respective mean. This procedure has been suggested by Smith and Sasaki (1979) as one method of combatting multicollinearity within the data when including both direct and interactive effects within the same regression model.

Computerized reservations systems (CRS) was coded 1 if the firm owned a major computerized reservations system (e.g., SABRE, APOLLO, WORLDSPAN, SYSTEM ONE, DATAS II, PARS) and 0 otherwise. This procedure also was used by Morrison and Winston (1995), but attention to CRS was excluded in all of the studies of competitiveness in the airline industry by Chen and colleagues (cf., Chen & Hambrick, 1995; Miller & Chen, 1996, 1994; Smith et al., 1991). Data for this measure came from the carriers' annual reports.

Organizational size (SIZE) was operationalized as the natural log of firm total assets. These data were taken from the COMPUSTAT PC Plus files.

Organizational performance was operationalized as the firm's operating profit margin, calculated as OPM = Operating profit/Operating revenue. This performance indicator was used by Morrison and Winston (1995) because it is insensitive to the firm's capital structure. With heavy debt financing among most of the carriers, this measure is a cleaner measure more comparable across firms. This measure was calculated from data included in the *Air Carrier Financial Statistics Quarterly* provided as a required filing by air carriers to the Department of Transportation.

Data Analysis

The regression equation was modeled using pooled, cross-sectional time series data with correction for autocorrelation and heteroskedasticity (Kmenta, 1971). Pooled, cross-sectional time series analyses have been used extensively by Chen and colleagues (cf., Miller & Chen, 1994, 1996; Smith et al., 1991) to consider performance effects of competitive action, and have also been used by Hansen and Hill (1991) to model the effects of institutional ownership on investment in research and development. Furthermore, this approach enables greater confidence in results than single year, cross-sectional studies (Dess, Gupta, Hennart, & Hill, 1995).

The equation testing the hypothesized antecedents to organizational performance, including the expected signs for each of the coefficients, was: $OPM_t = ICOOPOUT_t(+) + ED + INTERACT(ED*ICOOPOUT) + EM_t(+) + EC_t(-) + CRS_t (+) + SIZE_t$. Environmental dynamism was included as a direct effect to ensure correct model specification (Lewis-Beck, 1980). Support was found for the hypotheses if the signs on the beta coefficients were in the predicted direction and significant at $p = .10$. With a sample size of 10 firms for 14 years, the resulting sample size was $N = 140$, which is large enough to detect a medium effect size at power $= .80$ and $\alpha = .05$ (Green, 1991). When the analyses were run by deleting the 1983 observations, the results remained qualitatively unchanged. Thus, given that the retention of the remaining year provided greater power in the analyses, data from all fourteen years were used.

As Kmenta (1971) notes, pooled time series data create special problems for analysis because they include disturbance terms related to the cross-sectional disturbance, time-related disturbance, and potentially a combination of both of these sources. The model for analysis is described as: $Y_{it} = a_{it} + b_1X_{it,1} + b_2X_{it,2} + .. b_KX_{it,K} + \varepsilon_{it}$, where $i = 1,2, \ldots 10$ airlines, $t = 1,2, .. T$ years, and $K = 1,2, \ldots K$ independent variables. This study assumed that the autoregressive structure was homothetic across firms, in that $\varepsilon_t = \rho\varepsilon_{t-1} + u_t$, where ε is the error term, t is the time period, ρ is the autocorrelation between the errors, and u is the residual. Kmenta's (1971, p. 509-512) correction for autocorrelation was applied to the equations testing each performance variable. This correction ($^\wedge\rho$) was calculated with $\varepsilon_t = {}^\wedge\rho\varepsilon_{t-1} + u_t$, with ε the residual from the OLS equation for each performance variable, t the time period, and u the residual of this equation. Each dependent and independent variable was then adjusted.

To avoid throwing away an entire year's observations, Kmenta (1971) suggested that a correcting estimate of the autocorrelation ($^\wedge\rho$) could be derived for the first year of the data (for which the previous year's information is unavailable). Therefore, the adjustment for the dependent and independent variables for 1983 (the first year's data) used the following equation: $K_{adj,\ 1983} = \sqrt{(1 - (\rho^2))} * K$ For the years 1984-1996, the adjustment for autocorrelation used the following equation: $K_{Adj.,t} = K_t - {}^\wedge\rho K_{t-1}$, where $^\wedge\rho$ is the estimate of autocorrelation (ρ) taken from the estimation procedure described above, K is 1, 2, ... K independent and dependent variables, and T = 1,2, . . . T time periods. Inspection of the Durbin-Watson statistics for the equation after the adjustment indicated very limited remaining autocorrelation.

After the adjustment for autocorrelation, the t-ratios on the estimates for each of the independent variables were adjusted to control for heteroskedasticity with White's (1980) formula: $t = b/s$, where b is the unstandardized beta coefficient from the OLS regressions on the performance variables, and s is the square root of the respective variable's variance taken from the consistent covariance matrix (ACOV) from SAS. Hansen and Hill (1991) and Miller and Chen (1994) used similar approaches in their pooled, cross-sectional time series analyses.

RESULTS

Means, standard deviations, and bivariate correlations are presented in Table 1. Table 2 presents the results of the pooled, cross-sectional time series regression of operating profit margin on environmental and firm characteristics. The results of the analyses indicate support for several of the hypotheses. The R^2 for the equation was .24 (Adjusted R^2 = .20), and the F-ratio of 5.582 was significant at $p < .001$. Hypothesis 1 was not supported. The coefficient was small relative to its standard error, and the sign on the coefficient was in the opposite direction hypothesized. Therefore, there was no direct evidence that greater cooperative activity with firms outside the U.S. domestic airline industry contributed directly to increased operating performance. This result provides some support for the contention of Lado et al., (1997) that higher levels of cooperative strategies, in general, may be associated with only short-term gains.

However, the interactive effect of both intensity of cooperative relationships outside the U.S. domestic airline industry and environmental conditions

TABLE 1. Descriptive Statistics

Variable	Mean	S.D.	Correlations						
			1	2	3	4	5	6	7
1. OPM	.028	.069	1.00						
2. Size	3.509	.472	.07	1.00					
3. CRS	.636	.483	−.24**	.78***	1.00				
4. Environmental Munificence	.067	.040	.24**	−.13+	−.03	1.00			
5. Environmental Complexity	3.640	1.327	−.08	.70***	−.46***	.13+	1.00		
6. Environmental Dynamism	.044	.015	−.08	.22**	−.08	.11+	.21**	1.00	
7. Intensity of Cooperative Moves Outside Industry	.691	.041	−.08	.53***	.58***	.01	−.23**	−.01	1.00

N = 140 Significance levels reported are one–tailed.

*** $p < .001$

** $p < .01$

* $p < .05$

+ $p < .10$

TABLE 2. Results of Regression of Operating Profit Margin (OPM) on Company and Environmental Characteristics

Variable	β
Size	.579***
CRS	−.661***
Environmental Munificence (EM)	.179***
Environmental Complexity (EC)	−.096
Environmental Dynamism (ED)	.022
Intensity of Outside Cooperative Moves (ICOOPOUT)	−.009
Interaction (ED * ICOOPOUT)	.156**
R^2/ Adj. R^2	.24 / .20
F-ratio	5.852***
N	140

Standardized betas are shown for all coefficients.

*** $p < .001$

** $p < .01$

was supported in Hypothesis 2 ($p < .01$), indicating that under periods of increasing volatility within the airline industry, higher intensity of cooperative relationships outside the U.S. domestic airline industry was related to better performance. Therefore, as firms are faced with great variability in performance among fellow carriers, developing cooperative ventures outside the airline industry may be helpful ways to anchor their own performance within the industry. Such relationships may enable firms to retain customers, increase perceived switching costs, appear as a much more integrated travel network, gain perceived centrality and therefore greater support in the marketplace (Emerson, 1972; Grandori & Soda, 1995), or at least to reduce their own marketing and/or operations costs over the dynamic time periods.

Hypothesis 3 was also strongly supported ($p < .001$), with growing periods of opportunity within the airline industry raising performance across the board. Growth in unmet demand provided opportunities for all airlines to benefit without aggressively competing prices charged and benefits gained down to equilibrium.

Two hypotheses were not supported. Hypothesis 4 was not supported, though the sign on the coefficient was in the predicted direction. The exploratory Hypothesis 5 was not supported. In fact, the sign on the coefficient was negative, and the coefficient was large relative to its standard error. This result suggests that incidence of a major computerized reservations system alone did not contribute to operating performance, and perhaps the increased costs associated with maintenance of the systems do not outweigh the increased flexibility of more pliable organizational slack (Meyer, 1982). Morrison and Winston (1995) found that computerized reservations systems gave carriers important knowledge about consumer preferences and competitor actions, and also increased the firm's rate of return. Nevertheless, there are numerous examples of air carriers avoiding the demands of the major CRS providers, such as Southwest's unique development of electronic tickets to offset competitive pressures from American Airlines SABRE system in the mid-1990s. Further research will need to focus more extensive attention on this issue and the specific sources of advantage that accrue to carriers with large computerized reservations systems, especially as it has drawn great attention from legislative concerns.

Hypothesis 6 was strongly supported ($p < .001$), with size conveying benefits of economics of scale and scope as anticipated (Hurdle et al., 1989). Despite the largest losses in airline history that occurred during this study period, trends over the past decade have clearly forced carriers of all sizes to be more cost conscious, and those with the largest systems can be expected to benefit most actively from such measures. The following section presents a discussion of these results.

DISCUSSION

The central question of interest in this study was whether cooperative relationships with firms outside the U.S. domestic airline industry contributed to airline performance. The evidence from this pooled, cross-sectional time series analysis suggests that only under periods of environmental volatility do such relationships improve airline operating performance. These results suggest that further attention will need to be given to codifying the various types of cooperative alliances with firms outside the airline industry. This codification of non-airline alliances might follow levels of increasing complexity of shared resources, such as that advocated by Northwest's Michael Levine, with regard to airline cooperation: (1) alliance without a code share; (2) pro-rated code sharing; (3) code share and block space agreements; (4) shared revenue arrangements; and (5) highly integrated joint ventures (Oden, 1998). In any case, greater attention will need to be given to selecting the optimal collection of cooperative relationships to pursue so that firms do not overcommit themselves to too broad a variety of collaborative endeavors and thereby remove attention from direct competition (Lado et al., 1997) and overreliance on exploration instead of balancing between exploration and exploitation of existing opportunities (March, 1991).

Further research will also need to focus on the timing and implementation of these alliances. The present study only focuses on their announcement, and due to the lack of available data, does not follow through on an intensive critical evaluation of each of the alliances. Care must be taken with the generalizability of these results, since the performance implications were only evaluated for U.S. carriers. Do these relationships also hold for global carriers? Is the nature of the relationship similar, or are there different factors in other national and cultural environments that affect the role of cooperative relationships in firm performance? Finally, performance in the present study was operationalized only with operating profit margin. Future research will need to more broadly conceptualize the performance construct and to identify how and when cooperative relationships outside the industry contribute to improvements in performance relative to competitors.

This study is the first of its kind to explicitly test the performance effects of cross-industry cooperative alliances in the airline industry. The results present interesting questions for future research to build upon, both in the airline industry and in other industries. For example, how can cooperative alliances be categorized with regard to their performance implications and/or implementation challenges (e.g., resource sharing, complexity of governance, etc.)? Important beginnings on the generic nature of cooperative alliances has been made by Smith, Carroll, and Ashford (1995), but further research is needed on the specific rationale and coordinating mechanisms associated with cross-industry collaboration (Gulati, 1995). Second, how specifically do these different types of alliances contribute to organizational performance? Given the integration challenges notable across alliances and joint ventures of numerous types, what formal and informal filtering mechanisms can companies initiate to provide greater certainty of the positive outcomes of such cooperation? Finally, do different business-level strategies imply diverse approaches to the use of cooperative alliances outside the focal industry? This study provides an initial look at the potential for cross-industry cooperative alliances to contribute to organizational performance, and it is hoped that future research will more clearly delineate these contributions.

REFERENCES

_____. 1992. *Fewer Airlines, Higher Fares.* Hearing Before the Adhoc Subcommittee on Consumer and Environmental Affairs of the Committee on Governmental Affairs. U.S. Senate, 102th Congress. February 21. Washington, DC: USGPO.

Adelman, M.A. 1969. Comment on the'H' concentration measure as a numbers-equivalent. *Review of Economics and Statistics*, 51: 99-101.

Aldrich, H., & Whetten, D.A. 1981. Organization-sets, action-sets, and networks: Making the most of simplicity. In Nystrom, P.C. & Starbuck, W.H. (eds.), *Handbook of Organizational Design. Volume 1: Adapting Organizations to Their Environments*. Oxford: Oxford University Press: 385-408.

Astley, W.G., & Fombrun, C.J. 1983. Collective strategy: Social ecology of organizational environments. *Academy of Management Review*, 8, 4: 576-587.

Baum, J.A.C. 1996. Organizational ecology. In Glegg, S. et al. (eds.), *Handbook of Organization Studies*. London: Sage: 77-114.

Brandenburger, A.M., & Nalebuff, B.J. 1995. The right game: Use game theory to shape strategy. *Harvard Business Review*, 73, 4: 57-71.

Brandenburger, A.M., & Nalebuff, B.J. 1996. *Co-opetition*. New York: Doubleday.

Bresser, R.K.F. 1988. Matching collective and competitive strategies. *Strategic Management Journal*, 9: 375-385.

Browne, W.G., Toh, R.S., & Hu, M.Y. 1995. Frequent flier programs: The Australian experience. *Transportation Journal*, 35, 2: 35-44.

Buckley, P.J., & Casson, M. 1988. A theory of cooperation in international business. In F.J. Contractor & P. Lorange (Eds.), *Cooperative Strategies in International Business*: 31-53. Lexington, MA: Lexington Books.

Castrogiovanni, G.J. 1991. Environmental munificence: A theoretical assessment. *Academy of Management Review*, 16, 3: 542-565.

Chen, M.-J. 1996. Competitor analysis and interfirm rivalry: Toward a theoretical integration. *Academy of Management Review*, 21, 1: 100-134.

Chen, M.-J., & Hambrick, D.C. 1995. Speed, stealth, and selective attack: How small firms differ from large firms in competitive behavior. *Academy of Management Journal*, 38,2: 453-482.

Chen, M.-J., & MacMillan, I.C. 1992. Nonresponse and delayed response in competitive moves: The roles of competitor dependence and action irreversibility. *Academy of Management Journal*, 35: 539-570.

Chen, M.J., & Miller, D. 1994. Competitive attack, retaliation, and performance. *Strategic Management Journal*, 15, 2: 85-102.

Chen, M.-J., Smith, K.G., & Grimm, C.M. 1992. Action characteristics as predictors of competitive responses. *Management Science*, 38: 439-455.

Das, T.K., & Teng, B.-S. 1998. Between trust and control: Developing confidence in partner cooperation in alliances. *Academy of Management Review*, 23, 3: 491-512.

Department of Transportation. 1994. *FAA Statistical Handbook of Aviation.* Washington, DC; U.S. Department of Commerce, National Technical Information Service.

Dess, G., Gupta, A., Hennart, J.F., & Hill, C.W.L. 1995. Conducting and integrating strategy research at the international, corporate, and business-levels: Issues & directions. *Journal of Management,* 21, 3: 357-393.

Dess, G.G., & Beard, D.W. 1984. Dimensions of organizational task environments. *Administrative Science Quarterly,* 29: 52-73.

Doz, Y.L. 1996. The evolution of cooperation in strategic alliances: Initial conditions or learning processes? *Strategic Management Journal,* 17 (Summer Special Issue): 55-83.

Emerson, R.M. 1972. Exchange theory, Part II: Exchange relations and networks. In Rosenberg, M., and R. Turner (eds.), *Social Psychology: Social Perspectives.* New York: Academic Press: 30-65.

Grandori, A., & Soda, G. 1995. Inter-firm networks: Antecedents, mechanisms, and forms. *Organization Studies,* 16, 2: 183-214.

Granovetter, M. 1985. Economic action and social structure: The problem of embeddedness. *American Journal of Sociology,* 91, 3: 481-510.

Green, S.B. 1991. How many subjects does it take to do a regression analysis? *Multivariate Behavioral Research,* 26, 3: 499-510.

Gulati, R. 1995. Social structure and alliance formation patterns: A longitudinal analysis. *Administrative Science Quarterly,* 40, 4: 619-652.

Hansen, G.S., & Hill, C.W.L. 1991. Are institutional investors myopic? A time-series study of four technology-driven industries. *Strategic Management Journal,* 12, 1: 1-16.

Hurdle, G.J., Johnson, R.L., Joskow, A.S., Werden, G.J., & Williams, M.A. 1989. Concentration, potential entry, and performance in the airline industry. *The Journal of Industrial Economics,* 38, 2: 119-139.

Ingram, P., & Inman, C. 1996. Institutions, intergroup competition, and the evolution of hotel populations around Niagara Falls. *Administrative Science Quarterly,* 41, 4: 629-658.

Jarillo, J.C. 1988. On strategic networks. *Strategic Management Journal,* 9, 1: 31-41.

Jaworski, B.J., & Kohli, A.K. 1993. Market orientation: Antecedents and consequences. *Journal of Marketing,* 57, 53-70.

Kmenta, J. 1971. *Elements of econometrics.* New York: MacMillan.

Kohli, A.K., & Jaworski, B.J. 1990. Market orientation: The construct, research propositions, and managerial implications. *Journal of Marketing,* 54, 1: 1-18.

Krippendorff, K. 1980. Content analysis: An introduction to its methodology. Beverly Hills: Sage.

Kwandwalla, P.N. 1981. Properties of competing organizations. In Nystrom, P.C. & Starbuck, W.H. (Eds.), *Handbook of Organizational Design. Volume 1: Adapting Organizations to Their Environments.* Oxford: Oxford University Press: 409-432.

Lado, A.A., Boyd, N.G., & Hanlon, S.C. 1997. Competition, cooperation, and the search for economic rents: A syncretic model. *Academy of Management Review,* 22, 1: 110-141.

Levine, M.E. 1987. Airline competition in deregulated markets: Theory, firm strategy, and public policy. *Yale Journal on Regulation*, 4, 2: 393-494.

Lewis-Beck, M.S. 1980. *Applied regression: An introduction.* Sage University Paper series on Quantitative Applications in the Social Sciences, series no. 07-022. Newbury Park, CA: Sage.

March, J.G. 1991. Exploration and exploitation in organizational learning. *Organization Science*, 2, 1: 71-87.

Maxon, R. 1996. Sharing a ride: Airlines eagerly form flight alliances. *The Dallas Morning News*, May 9, 1D.

Meyer, A.D. 1982. Adapting to environmental jolts. *Administrative Science Quarterly*, 27: 515-537.

Miller, D., & Chen, M.-J. 1994. Sources and consequences of competitive inertia: A study of the U.S. airline industry. *Administrative Science Quarterly*, 39: 1-23.

Miller, D., & Chen, M.-J. 1996. The simplicity of competitive repertoires: An empirical analysis. *Strategic Management Journal*, 17, 6: 419-439.

Mitchell, W., & Singh, K. 1996. Survival of businesses using collaborative relationships to commercialize complex goods. *Strategic Management Journal*, 17: 169-195.

Morrison, S.A., & Winston, C. 1995. *The evolution of the airline industry.* Washington, DC: The Brookings Institution.

Nielsen, R.P. 1988. Cooperative strategy. *Strategic Management Journal*, 9: 475-492.

Nitko, A.J. 1983. Reliability of test scores. In A.J. Nitko, ed., *Educational Tests and Measurement: An Introduction.* New York: Harcourt, Brace, Jovanovich and Co.: 387-408.

Oden, J. 1998. Air alliances as growth engines: Alliances among airlines–such as the one Northwest now has with KLM and will have with Continental–smooth the way for expanded services and higher profits. *Saint Paul Pioneer Press*, February 15: 1D.

Oster, C.V., Jr., & Pickrell, D.H. 1986. Marketing alliances and competitive strategy in the airline industry. *Logistics and Transportation*, 22, 4, pp. 371-387.

Pfeffer, J., & Nowak, P. 1976. Joint ventures and interorganizational interdependence. *Administrative Science Quarterly*, 21: 398-418.

Powell, W.W., Koput, K.W., & Smith-Doerr, L. 1996. Interorganizational collaboration and the locus of innovation: Networks of learning in biotechnology. *Administrative Science Quarterly*, 41, 1: 116-145.

Provan, K. 1982. Interorganizational linkages, and influence over decision marketing. *Academy of Management Review*, 25, 2: 443-452.

Ring, P.S., & Van de Ven, A.H. 1994. Developmental processes of cooperative interorganizational relationships. *Academy of Management Review*, 19, 1: 90-118.

Scherer, F.M. 1970. *Industrial market structure and economic performance.* Chicago: Rand McNally and Co.

Smith, K.G, Carroll, S.J., & Ashford, S.J. 1995. Intra- and interorganizational cooperation: Toward a research agenda. *Academy of Management Journal* 38, 1: 7-23.

Smith, K.G., Grimm, C.M., Gannon, M.J., & Chen, M.-J. 1991. Organizational information processing, competitive responses, and performance in the domestic airline industry. *Academy of Management Journal*, 34, 1: 60-85.

Smith, K.W., & Sasaki, M. (1979). Decreasing multicollinearity: A method for models with multiplicative functions. *Sociological Methods and Research*, 8, 1: 35-56.

Teece, D.J. 1992. Competition, cooperation, and innovation: Organizational arrangements for regimes of rapid technological progress. *Journal of Economic Behavior and Organization*, 18: 1-25.

Thompson, J.D. 1967. *Organizations in Action*. New York: McGraw-Hill.

Thorelli, H.B. 1986. Networks: Between markets and hierarchies. *Strategic Management Journal*, 7: 37-51.

Venkataraman, S., Chen, M.-J., & MacMillan, I.C. 1997. Anticipating reactions: Factors that shape competitor responses. In Day, G.S. & Reibstein, D.J., (eds.), with R.E. Gunther, *Wharton on Dynamic Competitive Strategy*. New York: John Wiley and Sons: 198-219.

White, H. (1980). A heteroskedasticity-consistent covariance matrix estimator and a direct test for heteroskedasticity. *Ekonometrika*, 48, 817-838.

Index